SERVING THE SPIRITS:

THE RELIGION OF VODOU

by

Bon Mambo Vye Zo Komande LaMenfo

(Patricia Scheu)

For Donald – My North Star, partner and love.

I promised you'd never be bored.

Acknowledgements

There are always too many folks involved in any story to thank properly, but let me start with Lisa Chavez Maier, my editor, who took me through several drafts with her elegant style and always helpful encouragement. I doubt this book would be here today without her generous support, words of encouragement and the look that always told the truth of my writing. I also want to thank my brother Joseph Diorio for tirelessly answering my questions about grammar, sentence structure and helping me navigate the mysteries of the written English language. I am blessed to be surrounded by bright creative people and I would be a fool not to call on their expertise when needed. So a big thanks goes out to Dr. Yvonne Chireau for her insightful reading and thoughtful commentary on the original manuscript. When he was not keeping the beat of our fets in time, Professor James Armstrong generously helped correct all my drum rhythms. Dr. Eoghan Ballard was instrumental in checking all my Kongo material and discussing African ideas of cosmology with me. I also want to give thanks to all the beloved members of La Sosyete du Marche who were my think tank for the past ten years of teachings, ceremonies and services. Vodou is a blend of cultures and people and that is very true of our own sosyete as well. We have had many people who joined us in the dance beneath our tonnel over the years and lent their ashe to our work. Mesi anpil to the Haitian priests who taught me what I know - Bon Houngan Fritzner Georges, Bon Houngan

Edgar Jean Louis and Bon Houngan Lazireau Lerine, I stand tall on your shoulders today. To those members of the Haitian community who opened their homes and hearts to me, I cannot say thank you enough for all the kindnesses shown -- Leonine Hermantine, Mahalia Stines, Richard and Lunise Morse, Joel Ambroise and Mercedes Garcia, Mambo Jolie and her wonderful La Sosyete Sen Charles Borromeo. A *gran mesi anpil* to my godson Bon Houngan Nicodem Lazaro and his family -- his beautiful wife Manbo Nancy, his sister Manbo Gladys and their beloved Mammi Val, for all the songs, dances, services and help with my kreyol. I would also like to thank all the American Vodouisants who shared their temples, time and knowledge with me over the years -- my mother Mambo Shakmah Winndrum and my family in the New SEED Sanctuary; Mother Miriam Chamani and the Voodoo Temple; Mambo Sallie Ann Glassman and all the members of La Source Ancienne Ounfo; my spiritual siblings Mambo Kineta Chein and Houngan Julian Burnet. A special thanks goes to my spiritual brother Babalawo Fa'Ja'Na' Harden and his husband Robert Pouliot for all their support, late night phone calls and energy as I learned to walk this path. And finally to the ancestors both near and far -- Mom and Dad, the Italian *familia*, the Canadian *clique*, the German *kaffe klatch* and the African *society* -- I give thanks for your courage, your strength and your guidance. I love you all more than I can ever express. Ayibobo.

Contents

An Introduction

"There are as many Lwa as there are stars in the sky," my kanzo papa Bon Houngan Fritzner George told me one day during my training to become a priest of Vodou. As I watched the proceedings of a Vodou dance unfold for us that evening, I could see in person what he had spoken of earlier.

Standing on the *pe*, the circular altar that surrounded the center pole of the temple, a tiny mambo danced elaborate circles round and round the elevation, the Lwa Ezili Freda in her head. Below her on the ground, three hounsi were slithering about in full possession by Ezili's husband Danbala. And on the opposite side of the temple, a man called for rum and a machete as the Lwa Ogoun descended to take his place in the hierarchy of spirits roaming the peristyle space that evening. Despite their stellar origins, the stars that had fallen into the temple space were expressing themselves in very human terms. Servitors were running for offerings, clothing and food to share with these luminaries who had chosen to visit us. Rum, tobacco and perfume were the preferred gifts that were liberally shared with everyone present, spirits and human alike. As the evening came to its end the Lwa retreated, leaving behind advice, blessings and very tired "*chwals*"- the term used to describe a servitor under possession. Papa nodded with great satisfaction as the last of the Lwa left a hounsi sitting slightly dazed in a corner.

"The Spirits are very pleased that you are here," he said, as the drummers kept a danceable rhythm going. "They came in abundance to see you! Tomorrow, it will be your turn!"

I smiled uneasily back, not sure if I was ready to be *chawl* or just observer. But one thing I was sure of, I was in Haiti to become Mambo Asogwe, the rank of service in the faith. And I was determined to help change the worldview of Vodou along the way.

Vodou is not a cult, a magical means for personal gain, or any of the Hollywood stereotypes. It is a religious practice, a faith that points toward intimate knowledge of God, and offers its practitioners a means to come into communion with the Divine, through an ever evolving paradigm of dance, song and prayers. It is an invocation wrought from skin – hands, drums and feet, in joyous pounding prayers that brings Heaven down to earth. Vodou helps to explain the mysteries around us, and to express the many truths of the world through song, dance and drum rhythms. Vodou has helped me express who I really am and has given me a profound sense of purpose in life. My morning prayers, my afternoon services and my pastoral counseling form my daily routines. I spend my free time creating artwork in service to the Lwa, the great Mysteries that are served under God. I learn their songs and drum beats and dance before my altars for them, to share my laughter and my sense of accomplishment. Vodou has given substance and shape to my life and I am deeply grateful for all that I have. I find immense satisfaction in expressing myself as a mambo or "mother of the spirits."

There are many ways you can express your inner sense of self. Fashion is one system. Group affiliation is another, whether it's a social or religious group. Religion is perhaps one of the most personal ways to finding your place in the world. To fully give yourself over to a religion, it helps to understand the history and circumstances that gave birth to that religion. All faiths reflect the morals and rules of the societies that give rise to them. The myths of Christianity, from the "virgin birth" to the crucifixion of the Christ, perfectly reflect the laws of the ancient world that gave rise to it. The books of the Torah reflect back the society of Judaism at its inception. And the rules of the Koran speak to the time when the Prophet Mohammed walked on earth.

Vodou is no exception. The ceremonies, songs and liturgy of Vodou clearly demonstrate the mix of African nations and their religious ideas and practices that contributed to what we now know as modern Vodou. In each region of Haiti, we can trace the original African nations by listening to the various drum beats and songs played for a Vodou ceremony. At any given service, you can hear Colonial contradanses and African yanvalous performed side by side, dressed in Caribbean colors, with European accents.

This intermixing of nations – African, European and Caribbean -- is the legacy left to us by the Ancient Africans. Their gift to Vodou is clearly demonstrated through its liturgy – everyone is included; no one is excluded.

My late Gran'n Papa Kanzo, Bon Houngan Luc Gédéon always insisted every person is welcome in Vodou, because every person has a Lwa met tet, every person has ancestors. In every country there are crossroads - that is the Lwa Kafou. In every country there are woods where ancient Grand Bwa resides. Every race of people produces twins that the Haitians call Marassa. These are the basics of Vodou, found all over the world, in every place, culture and village of humanity. As the Fon people of West Africa say, everything is Vodou; there is nothing that isn't Vodou. That is because the word Vodou means spirit in their language. To the ancient Africans, they saw Spirit as being immanent in all things under heaven.

The saying is "Vodou includes, it does not exclude." That gives meaning to the fact that Haitian Vodou has its roots in many African ethnic groups, including the afore mentioned Fon (of West Africa), the Dahomeans (who live in what is now called Benin), and Yorubans (who live in what is now called Nigeria). Vodou also draws from the rich and diverse Kongo people: the Ibos, Senegal and Kapalou nations. We remember these and the other plantation era Africans as the 21 nations of Vodou. These various nations of people lent names of spirits, drumming rhythms, dance footsteps, and many forgotten words (*langaj*) to the mélange we know today as Haitian Vodou.

Although the African root is deep and prominent, Vodou also combines elements from the colonial plantation era into its bricolage. The plantation owners were French, Spanish and Dutch, and came out of a time when the Enlightenment was just beginning to make its mark in thinking, in science and in mystical practices such as Kabala. Catholicism added its own touches through the synchronicity of Catholic hagiography (the saints, their images and their stories.). British sailing lore lent the use of model ships and colorful flags. And finally, the occultism of European Masonry, the mysticism of the Spanish Cabalists and European folk practices such as carnival parades at Lent all seasoned the brew that became modern day Vodou.

As an example of this accumulative nature, at the start of every service the presiding mambo or houngan sings the Priye Ginen, the Prayer of Africa. A long recitation of the many spirits that are honored in a given sosyete, the Priye is the foundational prayer of Vodou. Everyone who is a servitor is expected to know the Priye by heart and to join in when it is sung for service. In that prayer, verses are sung for the Nigerian Papa Loko, for the Dahomean Houngan Agassou, for the Portuguese Don Pedro, for the Kongo Simbi Andezo, and for the Roman Catholic-derived Grand Saint Anne, who in her physical life was a Palestinian Jew. Racial prejudice and ethnic scorn are diametrically opposed to the agglomerative and inclusive tendency of Vodou.

If you compare the theology of religions such as Hinduism, Egyptian, Greek, Roman, you will find incredible similarities between them. They all espouse one supreme creator who created a multiple pantheon of otherworldly spirits who act as servants to both Man and God. Even the Old Testament of the Bible shows multiple pantheons of Angels (Seraphim, Watchers, etc.) as well as animal sacrifice, including human sacrifice. These religions in their oldest forms share a similar set of paradigms used to help their congregations: prayers of invocation, songs of praise and morality tales that feature heroes and villains, beautiful maidens and powerful warriors. These individuals are all vying for attention, adoration and veneration, so They can receive the greatest reward possible – that of serving Their Creator to the fullest capacity of Their own potential.

This competition for attention and adoration comes with the price of service by the humans, but also with the reward of enlightenment for those who can see the Divine spark in the actions of the spirits. Such feats of attention are meant to be examples of how one can live in the world, with the result being a balanced and harmonious life. We accept these examples as proof that the Divine has a plan and can bring about knowledge of our own Divine nature. But it is the lives of the spirits, those maidens and warriors that reflect our own inner divinity that we seek. By studying their exploits, emulating their choices and learning from their mistakes, we can find the Divine in all we do in this mundane life. That is another gift of Vodou – finding our own Divinity, by seeking its reflection in the lives and loves of the Lwa.

The Divine shows Him/Herself to each culture in a way that the culture can understand, have faith in and incorporate into its daily life in the context of which they circumstantially live. In other words, the religion reflects the society that gave rise to it. Just as in the Old Testament, where God's voice/ message was heard through Angels, in Vodou those Angels are called Lwa. You learn their names, their purpose, their preferred offerings and ways to engage with them for the betterment of yourself, your family and your community. In return, the Lwa and their stories offer wisdom, guidance, and inspiration for you to draw upon daily.

There is no doctrine in Vodou, no dogma, no "pope" of Vodou. Each sosyete or house is its own autonomous collective. But underscoring all Vodou sosyetes (the name of the family centric groups of worshippers) is what is known as *Reglemen* – the order of service, songs and drum beats; the manner in which rituals and ceremonies are performed; the dances that are offered to the Lwa for their entertainment and pleasure. Depending on where on the island you go, the services are similar, yet different, reflecting the makeup of the African populations from ancient times. Along with the dominant styles of a given location, the Spirits themselves have their own styles, wants and desires, making these things known among the servitors of a particular house. These wishes are then incorporated into the dances, the praise poems and vèvè, giving each Vodou sosyete its own particular stylistic take on the Reglemen of Vodou. Thus, when speaking of Vodou, one cannot find a rigid system of belief, because to do so would exclude the very soul of the religion and its colorful, inclusive nature. Vodou includes, it does not exclude.

Vodou is not magic, but it does offer a path in which you can physically touch God and the Lwa. That is what brought me to the faith: proof, in physical form, that God lives and is willing to personally show His face to me through His messengers, the Lwa. I like a religion that allows me to have conversation with the angels. But you have got to have faith that what you think you know about Vodou isn't the entire story.

In order for you to give yourself over to the beauty inherent in Vodou, you must first forget what the media and society has drilled into the public consciousness - that Vodou is evil, diabolic or just plain old hocus-pocus. Secondly, you must learn the history of Haiti, the Sugar Kingdom of the Caribbean and home of the enslaved Africans who came to create this faith for themselves. The remarkable gift of Vodou was to create a religion that 21 diverse nations of people could understand, grasp and more importantly, believe in wholeheartedly. No other religion can make this claim of unity through diversity. Finally, clear your head, make a commitment to yourself that this path is relevant to your life, and have faith.

This book is a beginner's primer on Vodou. It was not my intent for it to be the final word on the faith, nor is it the most common set of practices. Rather, it is one sosyete's method of working the Reglemen of Vodou. There are many others. I am aware of being a "blan" mambo, and I work very hard to keep our liturgical practices as real as I possibly can, so that I do not acculturate the faith. My godkids are taught this as well, and together we strive to follow the tenets of the faith. To this end, I have created an extensive resource list for you to help broaden your knowledge of Vodou and its methodologies.

I will try to explain to you the high points of Vodou as I work with them daily. I am a mambo asogwe – the highest rank that one can hold in Vodou. It is the rank of service – to the spirits, to my sosyete and to the community at large. It is my oath as a priest to be of service. I make this book an offering to Legba, the great gate keeper, to open the way for your journey – that it may be filled with wonder, awe and inspiration. That you find the truth you seek. And that together we become more than author and reader but family, as Vodou has always done: uniting strangers in faith, making families out of people who are not related by blood, but by respect, honor and most importantly love.

Mambo Vye Zo Komande La Menfo Daginen

Chapter One: A Short History of Haiti

In Vodou, we like to say that in order to know where you are going, you must see where you have been. So let us begin with a little geography in the Caribbean.

Haiti is the western half of the island known as Hispaniola. The other half is the Dominican Republic. Since the 2010 earthquake, more people are aware of the island than ever before. Before the earthquake, I would tell people about Haiti and the first question was always, "Where is it?". People were always amazed when I drew the map and showed them just how close it is to our borders. For the record, Haiti lies east to west in the western Caribbean Sea, 90 miles off the southern tip of Cuba, opposite Guantanamo Bay. It is also a mere 19 degrees north of the Equator, making it a very tropical island. That heat and humidity was what made it the Sugar Bowl of the world for nearly 300 years.

All tropical islands are magical, but none more so than Haiti. Here, the aquamarine waters of the Caribbean kiss white sand beaches and palms trees sigh over the exchange. But that image is quite often at odds with the grinding poverty, burning hunger and relative isolation of its people. It is a very hard place – hilly and mountainous, often gray and overcrowded, its people rail thin and rock hard from their labors.

And yet, despite being hounded by world governments and international media as a dangerous place and having had its reputation shredded by the film industry, Haiti endures. Not just because of its remarkable people, but for its amazing faith in itself. Once called the Pearl of the Antilles, Haiti has suffered egregiously at the hands of the many for the profits of the few.

I return every year, because I can hear LaSiren's call beneath the squalor of Cite Soliel. Because even the roughest peasant has the manners of a Napoleonic courtier. Because I met Gran Bwa one night, out on a lush patch of pasture under a full moon, and He was the most amazing creature I have ever come across. Because as Tina Girouard wrote in her book, *Sequin Artists of Haiti* (1996), "Once you have gone to Haiti, you are forever Haitian in your soul." I also return, because on the island of Haiti, one is never alone, physically or spiritually.

Vodou spirits are omnipresent, omnipotent and omniscient in Haiti. In downtown Port au Prince, as you climb aboard the ubiquitous tap-tap there is Ogoun Feray offering a helping hand. Shop at the Marche Fey, and Vodou is everywhere – in every stall and under every awning. Travel the length and breadth of the island and wherever you look you see the imagery of Vodou painted on walls, on doors, on buses and taxis, even on the people themselves. There is simply no escaping from the Vodou.

I said earlier that Vodou includes, not excludes and that statement begins with the Native populations who were living here at the time of the invaders. The first known settlers of the island were the Ciboney Indians who migrated from what is currently the North American continent in 450 A.D. These people were followed in 900 A.D by the Tainos (meaning 'the good people') who were members of the Arawak nation and had origins in the Amazon valley. The Tainos were a peaceful agricultural people who lived in large villages also peopled by a small number of Caribs Indians who had emigrated from what is today South America. The Tainos called the island "Ayiti" which meant "land of mountains."

Today we have remnants of these cultures in the Petro division of Vodou rituals. The services of the Lwa like Don Pedro, Maynette, Ti-Jean and some variations of Dantor are tinged with Native influences through colors, service styles and drum beats. No anthropological sites remain in Haiti for us to study these cultures, but bits and pieces survive in the older lakous. Some of the oldest houngans living today remember their great grandparents as having Indian family members. And in the amazing home of Marianne Lehman, a Swiss ex-pat who has been an dedicated collector of Bizango and Vodou artefacts for 50 years, one finds the odd bit of Arawak or Taino history – a stone axe head, arrow heads and bone fetishes. These precious pieces of Haiti's past are all that remain of the natives who greeted the invaders at the northern tip of island.

In or around 1480, the Spanish had finished conquering the Iberian Peninsula and forcing the Moors out of Seville. Along with this thrashing, they also came to appreciate some of the cultural items they encountered as they fought with the Arabian Moors. Sugar was one of those items. Slavery was the other. Although we here in the west think of slavery as a Western affliction, the fact is it was a long held condition of human misery. Slavery was a well established practice in the Orient as well as the Mediterranean basin, but it took the addition of sugar to make slavery a viable Atlantic business trade.

With the Spanish Queen Isabella's blessing and financial backing, Christopher Columbus set out from Granada, Spain for the new world with three ships loaded not with guns but with sugar cane plants. After a three month voyage at sea, he landed at Port de Paix in Northern Haiti on December 5, 1492. In fact, when the Santa-Maria wrecked near the coast of what is today Cap-Haitien, the Arawaks were happy to help Columbus salvage the ship, carrying timber ashore. The timber was used to build the first European settlement in the 'New World': La Navidad (Nativity).

With permission from the local chief, Guacanagari[1], he left behind 39 men and established the town of LaNavidad. Before

---

1 Mclean, F. (2008, January 01). The lost fort of columbus. *Smithsonian Magazine*, Retrieved from http://www.smithsonianmag.com/history-archaeology/fort-of-columbus-200801.html.

setting sail back to Seville, he kidnapped ten to twenty-five local natives and took them back to display to Queen Isabella.

Although he was busy with his plans to return, Columbus did take a good look around and saw not the precious yellow metal of the Queen's dreams but earth so dark he called it black gold. He returned one year later with more ships, more men, 1500 cane shoots and 100 Moorish slaves to do the planting. These nameless men would begin to contribute their own culture to the early brew of Vodou. Today, we have Moslem words such as the greeting "As-salaam-Alaikum" heard in the north of Haiti when certain Lwa arrive. There are tiled floors in temples, reminiscent of Arabic mosques and a Lwa's boat named "Imammou". The cross-cultural integration of societies and Haiti had begun without any extant record other than a verbal memory of the addition. Haiti would never be the same.

Columbus returned to Spain to organize an even bigger expedition. Upon arriving at La Navidad, they found that the Caribs had taken over, destroying the fort and slaughtering all the Spanish and Taino within. Columbus abandoned the site, sailing East and established a colony in what is today the Dominican Republic. He came with the means to begin planting, carrying live cane shoots and the slaves to plant them. Gold was found in a nearby river, thereby dooming the island to Spanish exploitation and ruin.

The Spaniards weren't content with the gold – they also saw cheap labor in the Arawaks. They used any method to control the native populations – rape, murder and whippings, not to mention what measles, mumps and small pox did to them as well. This regime of terror led to the decimation of the local population of Native peoples. Estimates suggest that somewhere between 300,000 and one million natives died between 1492 and 1550. With the native population dwindling as well as the gold, the Spaniards abandoned their gold rush and pushed into the Yucatan peninsula of Mexico, to plunder Central and South America as they had Hispaniola.

Officially under Spanish rule, the island was an exhausted ruin by the early 1600s. By 1630 French and British buccaneers, (freelance pirates) had established a foot hold on the northern island of Tortuga and by 1644 had established a settlement near Port-de-Paix on the North shore of Haiti (Hispaniola). This passage of water between Jamaica and Florida soon became known as the Windward Passage. However, turnabout is fair play. As the Spanish sailed home with their ships loaded with South American gold, they had to run for their lives in these waters. The buccaneers would raid their treasure-laden ships, killing the crews and keeping the stolen gold.

The seizure of the northern land tip by the buccaneers and their constant raiding of Spanish ships eventually led the Crown of Spain to cede the Western third of the island to France through the Treaty of Ryswick (1697). This portion of the island was renamed Saint Domingue and later became `La République d'Haiti'.

The French saw a good thing and went for it. Though the Spanish had bled the gold from the country, there were other resources to be had – indigo and ebony and mahogany forests to name but a few. And the soil that had so enthralled Columbus also drew the French for agriculture – cotton, cocoa and coffee. And of course, sugar cane.

Sugar was a plantation owner's dream crop. Cane germinated in six days. The heat and humidity of the tropics, combined with the rich volcanic soil, helped sugar cane grow an astonishing foot a week, ready for harvest in six, prime cut in seven. Cutting was done around the clock, with no time off. Every able bodied slave was put to the field – some as young as six. It was back breaking work, because the cane had to be cut at the ground. The island flourished economically under French rule. Trade with the colony was valued at around 140 million dollars per year[2].

This astounding economical success was obtained at a terrible price – the blood and bondage of human slaves. Sugar was the coin of the world in the 1600's of the new world. There is an unofficial record of a British sugar plantation on the island of Barbados as early as 1580, but on the official record, the sugar plantations saw their full genesis in the mid 1600's[3]. Columbus landing on Haiti's northern peninsula was just the tip of the proverbial sugar mountain. The Dutch, the English and the French began planting sugar in earnest, and it grew in the West Indies for

---

[2] Sheridan, R. (1994). *Sugar and Slavery: An Economic History of the British West Indies, 1623-1775.* Kingston: University of the West Indies Press.

[3] Sharkey, N. December 11, 1988. *A Barbados Synagogue Is Reborn.* New York: New York Times

100 years after this landing, but records show they made it look like they'd been at it for 300, so great was the volume of sugar produced – and the loss of human lives who were worked to death to harvest it[4].

There are records that show for every birth, there were two deaths. The average age was young – we do not have any records to tell us how young, but the population was often weighted toward the very young – 18-21 and older folks who had survived the ocean voyage to the island but could no longer work for a variety of reasons[5]. These people often became overseerers, housemaids and cooks. They had the better jobs if you can call cooking for hundreds of people a good job. They ate slightly better, were clothed in hand offs and stayed out of the brutal Caribbean sun, though their lives were no less harsh for their positions. The records of plantations show that there was a huge slant in the numbers – often 400-500 slaves living and working on a plantation that encompassed only 10 or so whites. The wonder isn't why they revolted, but why not sooner?

Over the ensuing years, the Portuguese would bring millions of people from the Kongo, Ibo, Nago, Mandingue, Arada, Dahomea and other West African civilizations, out of their

---

[4] Heinl, M. & Heinl, N. (1996). *Written in Blood: the Story of the Haitian People*, University Press of America.
[5] Bay, E. *Wives of the Leopard: gender, politics and culture in the Kingdom of Dahomey.* University of Virginia Press, 1998

homeland, transport them under abominable conditions and sell them to be used as forced labor in the colony. Due to the deplorable and inhuman conditions of this life, the population of African slaves never rose above 350,000 people, despite nearly three million people being sold into bondage every year.

The intermingling of colonists and slaves also brought forth a third class of people known as *affranchise* or people of color. These people were the product of plantation masters and slave mistresses. By 1670, they were equal in number to their white fathers. Often raised with the master's white children, they were educated abroad, and came home looking for a fair share of their family's wealth. They were in a sense, freed slaves, though free only in spirit, but not in fact.

In 1685, as a sort of empty gesture of concern, Louis XIV established the Code Noir, a rule by which any free slave was to be granted fu'l French citizenship. However, it came with a price tag. The plantation masters were not going to quietly accept the Code Noir. There was too much money at stake in the islands. With the ratio of slaves to colonist hovering at one hundred to one, they decided that slaves freed by either gift or purchase would remain part of an underclass with the privilege of ownership, but without the right to vote, join the army, become a medical doctor or pharmacist, or sit in the colonists' section in church. In other words, they had freedom without anywhere to go.

Amidst all this rhetoric about freedom, voting and political posturing, both classes forgot about the enslaved Africans who outnumbered them all. With the toll on human lives so high, the record number of Africans who came into the island meant that at any given time the members of the slave population were a mere two to three months in bondage on the island. And they well remembered their roots and where they came from. The Africans stood silent, watching and waiting.

The news of the French Revolution of 1789, and of the `Déclaration des droits de l'homme' (Human Rights Declaration) brought new hopes to the slaves and *affranchise* of Saint Domingue. Colonists did not however take the news with much enthusiasm and did not apply the reforms to the colony. They stupidly thought the mulatto class would continue under their rule and that the Africans would not understand the declaration and would simply continue on as before. That they were so wrong is an indication of their own ignorance about the very people they surrounded themselves with.

The Africans were not stupid. They were fighters, military men and women. They were strong and intelligent. They spoke not only their own tongue, but French, Spanish, Italian, Portuguese and English. They stood silently in the shadows of dozens of dining rooms and banquet halls, serving food – and listening. They understood everything that was being said. The colonists thought them mere draft animals, who stood with plates or towels, waiting for a command. Had they even the slightest inkling of who was standing guard at dinner watching and listening, the smart colonialist would have run for their lives. But they did not.

The result of the declaration was a series of revolts, first by the people of color in 1790 - met with brutal repression - then by the slaves in 1791. There was a turning point for all that we remember to this day.

A slave who we only know of as Boukman Dutty is credited with organizing the repressed population of Africans into an army of consequence. This resulted in the destruction of the sugarcane plantations and the massacre of thousands of colonists. The act of organizing and encouraging the slaves into revolt is remembered even to this day as the Ceremony of Bwa Kayiman (Alligator Woods). But this was just the tip of the iceberg. As successful as this one revolt was, there was still trouble ahead.

The European business community was not about to lose its cash cow to a bunch of rabble rousers. Britain, forever wanting more than its gluttoness share of income, watched as the revolt between the colonists, slaves and France erupted. Seeing a chance to add to its landholdings, Britain invaded the island, hoping to quell the revolution and come out the winner of the sugar island. This had the strange reaction of causing the French to do an about turn, and join hands with the very slaves they were fighting.

On August 29, 1793, a French Commissioner named Sonothonax abolished slavery on the island and no one really knows why. Either he was radically anti-slavery or more likely, he wanted to have the 350,000 former slaves help the French push back the British invasion. This was auspicious for the Africans, because this is where the first black General of the Army emerged – Toussaint L'Ouverture.

L'Ouverture, a harrier and free man of colour since 1777, was a smart, learned man. He could read, was fluent in three languages and could write. But it was his ability to speak with the eloquence of a Rhodes Scholar that put him ahead of all the other freed Africans who also had schooling. When Toussaint L'Ouverture spoke, thousands listened, and more importantly, believed in what he had to say.

L'Ouverture formed a battalion of former slaves under the French flag and drove out the British invaders. For his courage and valour at the front, he was appointed governor of Saint Domingue. In 1801, Toussaint went on to conquer the Eastern part of Hispaniola, abolished slavery there, and installed himself as governor of the entire island. In two short, yet tumultuous years, Toussaint had done what the French and the British together couldn't – he united the island, drove out the colonists and abolished slavery.

L'Ouverture wrote to Napoleon, and asked to be recognized as governor, with all the pomp and privilege that title held. Bonaparte saw this as a threat to France's control of the island and sent his brother-in-law LeClerc, along with 20,000 well armed troops to the island. Their mission was to capture Toussaint and re-establish slavery in the colony. Toussaint was deceived into capture in 1802 and shipped to France where he died while imprisoned in a cold jail cell in the Jura Mountains.

Toussaint's allies Henri Christophe and Jean-Jacques Dessalines had also surrendered to the French but they remained on the island. History favors the fortunate and France was not one. LeClerc's army was well armed, but exhausted from Bonaparte's expeditions through North Africa. Some troops had endured three deployments and were looking to just go home. Tired, demoralized and now sent to the subtropics, the men were primed for failure on all fronts. They arrived in the Caribbean just after monsoon season, when the mosquito population had bloomed to its yearly high. This led to the men contracting yellow fever at an alarming rate. Combined with poor diets, heavy wool clothing that was not suited to the tropical humidity and their own immune systems virtually wiped out by the African strains of dysentery, cholera and dengue fever, the troops died by the dozens daily.

Added to this was the news that France was planning to reinstate slavery. That had to be the piece that dashed all the hopes for these Africans, who had fought so valiantly beside the French, only to find out they would be betrayed in the end. On November 18, 1803 under leadership of Christophe, the French were defeated at the famed Battle of Veritieres outside of what is today Cap-Haitien.

20,000 French soldiers may have come ashore at Cap Haitian, but one year later, 2,000 swam for their lives off that very same beach. Dessalines proclaimed the independence of the island on January 1, 1804 and gave it back its native name of 'Haiti'. The first republic in the world to be led by a person of African descent was thus born.

Their freedom was hard won, but there would be an even bigger price to pay – isolation. In the ensuing years, the institution of slavery would come and go, and the European community would try to keep its greedy finger in the export pie. Haiti would suffer endless rounds of dictators, insurgents and lack luster leadership. When the last of the French priests left in 1845, Haiti would find itself cut off from the world for 80 years. As punishment for having sought to toss off its shackles of bondage, the emerging American and older European communities turned their backs on the tiny fledging nation. Haiti was on its own.

And in that isolation, a strange thing happened. Though poverty, hunger, class division and all the ills of a modern society would get a foothold, so too would the comfort of a religion that sought to answer the questions we all struggle with. Why? Why had they been abandoned? First by their own country men who sold them into slavery and then by the Spanish, and finally by the French? And why were they left to their own devices?

There is a saying in Vodou – "The Spirit chooses who it wishes." Perhaps, the Spirit needed its voice to be heard. In the cacophony of war, peace talks and treaty terms, the Spirit doesn't have a voice. But in the quiet of a lakou yard, when the work of the field is done, and the drums talk, there the Spirit can speak. And more importantly, can be heard.

Chapter Two: A Creole Nation

In the last chapter, we talked about the revolution that birthed the nation of Haiti. We discussed how the Spanish , French and British came into the island, leaving behind their languages, dances and styles of dress. We also talked about the many African nations that made up the plantation era slaves, who contributed their rhythms, songs and languages. These same influences also contributed to the religion we know today as Haitian Vodou.

Vodou is first and foremost a family faith. It had its genesis in West Africa and came to the New World via Transatlantic Slave trade. At the dawn of that era, the island of Haiti was a melting pot of all the many nations, civilizations and cultures that came into the island. And like any good melting pot, amazing things resulted.

The first was language. The Africans did not speak one another's language. The Fon didn't speak Kongolese. The Djouha did not speak Dahomean. Yet, they were all under subjugation by the French. So the Africans took the language of the French masters and made it their own. Haitian Creole is French with African syntax. Language would beget conversation between all the differing nations of Africans. The shared pain of bondage would unite strangers into families. These familial unions produced understanding of individual cultures and spiritual practices.

This understanding would blossom into a unified vision of worship. Individual nations of Africans would put aside their differences and unite to survive. They began their long journey to freedom by uniting in faith. That is the first gift Vodou gave the world: an example of what happens when a group of diverse people decide to look at what unites them spiritually, rather than what divides them psychologically.

This unified vision of worship can be heard in the liturgy of Vodou. In each region of Haiti, we can trace the original African nations by listening to the drum beats and songs played for a local ceremony. This intermixing of African, European and Caribbean language, music and worship is the legacy left to us by the Ancient Africans. This intermixing is the second gift of Vodou. Everyone is included; no one is excluded.

Including everyone meant not only those who were present in the colony, but also those who were left behind in Africa. Inclusion would also come to mean everyone who died at the hands of the plantocracy, both in the colony and in Africa. Worship would begin by remembering those who had gone before, as well as those who were yet to come.

The work of Vodou is about remembrance, balance and healing. Everything supports those three pillars -- remembrance of who you are, who you came from and where you originated from; balance a cool head so that you can walk a middle path of harmony in life; heal those who need it the most, by bringing balance and harmony into their lives. In the painful grip of slavery, healing was a full time job.

Remembrance comes into Vodou through the Native Arawak, Taino and Carib cultures who were present at the discovery of the island. There are remnants of these found in the Petro side of Vodou. The whip, the whistle and the bull roarer are all left over from that ancient and long forgotten time. Rachel Beauvoir-Dominique says that one possible origin of the asson, the sacred rattle that is emblematic of priesthood, is from the Tainos. They worshipped Iroko, a vegetation deity with a maraca like instrument. Iroko is a possible source that may have transformed over the centuries into Papa Loko Attisou, the Vodou spirit of leaves.

The European plantation culture is still remembered first in the language. French is spoken in school, church and business, but Creole is used for everyday conversation. The many nations of Africans could not speak to one another, and so they chose the language of the masters to be theirs, only with a twist. Not everyone in Haiti today speaks French. It is still considered to be an elitist language. But everyone speaks Creole. In Herb Gold's book *"Haiti, Best Nightmare on Earth"*, he recounts how stunned he and his wife were when they overheard their girls speaking Creole like natives, while still struggling to learn French in school. Language belies relationship, intimacy and insider status. Just recently, I attended a Haitian event. Everyone was guardedly polite, until I responded in Creole to a request. After that, everyone warmed up to me. I was speaking the language of the 'family.'

Creole is the national tongue of Haiti, but depending on where you go in Haiti, it is very different. The Creole spoken in the Artibonite is different from that in Cap Haitian and still again, from the language one hears on the streets of Jacmel. In each town, the dominant African population lent its own words, accents and style to the Creole spoken locally.

We also find remnants of the plantation culture in the music. In Fond de Negres, on the Southern Peninsula of Haiti, the locals play French minuets, Spanish meringues and Polish polkas at their Sunday gatherings! These musical patchworks are not newly learned talents, but music that has been in the family for generations. Having intermarried with Polish, Spanish and French people, there are blue eyed Haitians, who speak Polish, dance the Minuet and cut cane on a regular basis. Only in Haiti, can you find such an interwoven society with no prejudice for any of it, and a total delight in the multi-layered family this kind of social interaction produces.

All these various nations of people – their languages, their drum beats, their songs and art - are what we find interwoven throughout the Vodou religion. A friend has often told me in jest that Vodou is all about fabric and I must agree. The military flags of the Nago nation are reflected in the use of sequin flags in a peristyle, the temple of Vodou. The dresses of the Rada service are an allusion to the royal houses of West Africa, with the use of all white material. And the mushoirs of the faithful, those shiny satin head wraps, are a call to the Lwa who are said to prefer bright, reflective surfaces.

The circular dances, the center post and the construction of a temple is a direct Kongo import. Every peristyle in the country, no matter how large or small has at the heart of their worship space a post called the poto mitan. An allegorical tree whose 'branches' reach into heaven and whose 'roots' grow deeply into the earth, the poto mitan is the highway by which the Lwa descend to earth to dance with us in service.

The drums are directly from the villages of Africa. Their voices (or tones) represent the many nations that are their root. Drums are considered sacred in Vodou, and have a special place in service. There are services to baptize drums, feed them and even send them on a mystical voyage back to Ginen, where they are believed to be consecrated for playing in service. Drums are considered so holy that there are temples dedicated strictly to their service and use. The Assento drum that is held in the temple at Badjio is a descendant of an earlier one but both were carved and created in Africa.

But not all of Vodou is related to its African root. The colourful dresses and robes of countryside Rara bands are a direct imitation of Carnival in Europe. With their bright patterns, handkerchief skirts and tasselled tops, the *major jonc* (leader)of a Rara is better dressed than most of his or her European counterparts.

These emblems of Vodou -- flags, drums, music and dress all share common ancestry. They give voice to the many nations of Africans who bled for Vodou over the years. And they are a reminder of where Vodou came from, and where it is are going.

The bondage of slavery was the impetus that birthed Vodou in Haiti. The common strife the Africans shared became the focus of their rituals and their faith. Vodou did not spring forth fully formed, but grew to include all these various peoples, beliefs and ideas. And it is the inclusive nature of Vodou that allowed it to survive and thrive, from slavery days to this modern age.

Chapter Three: The Art and Culture of Vodou

A Creole nation was born from the many nations of people who came into the island of Haiti. French, Spanish and Africans, as well as Native Americans would all add their own talents and gifts to the blend known today as Vodou. Let's talk for a moment about how they reconciled their differences and created a whole religious faith from scratch.

The early Haitians were very creative, in both the way they coaxed a meager living from the earth and in their manner of worship. They did not need large temples or fancy churches. There was no money or materials to create such places. So Haitians rendered their spiritual ideas with what they had on hand. Open spaces became their cathedrals. Trees such as the holy mapou became their altars. And they made stain glass windows out of fabric and sequins, chalices from empty liquor bottles and vestments out of burlap bags. These original Haitian works of spiritually inspired art were so exquisitely created the world rushed in again to get a piece of them. Only now, Haiti was ready for the 'invaders.'

Today, Vodou is Haiti's number one national export product. On a tiny island, where there is no real industry or industrialized farming, Vodou's religious art provides the much needed cash flow that helps Haitian families survive. Stop by any roadside market stand and along with the mangos and cane stalks you will probably find sequined bottles, carved gourds and the occasional painting or two. But these are not the only source of income to originate in the faith. *Rasin* or roots music is also where one finds Vodou songs and phrases, set to modern styles of music. It is a growing industry, popularized by singers such as Richard Morse of RAM and the late Leonard Fortune, known as Azor.

There is no bible of Vodou, no hierarchy, no governing body. In fact, depending on the number of people you speak with, you will find a plethora of information regarding Vodou, the Lwa and the practices of service to said Lwa. All Vodou temples are autonomous and run independent of one another. There is an 85-90% overlap in the liturgy, mainly with the Prayer of Africa or Priye Ginen as it is called.

But the real heart and soul of the religion is in its liturgical corpus of songs. It is in the songs that the theology of Vodou is carried. It was easy to hide this from the plantation managers. Singing a song about something called Gran Bwa (Big Woods) probably seemed pretty innocuous to the Big Boss. But to the faithful, they knew exactly who they were calling in. The houngans and mambos 300 years ago might have been subjugated but they were not uninspired. They carried the liturgy of the religion in their songs, through allegory and innuendo.

Today, "*rasin*" is one of the most popular forms of music to come out of Haiti in decades. Many musicians take their inspiration from Vodou's rhythms and beats. Richard Morse, leader of the progressive rock band known worldwide as RAM, is one example. Morse is Haitian-American and was drawn to the island to learn the musical beats. He became involved with Vodou, and his music is now one of the most popular ways folks learn the some of the songs from the Vodou corpus.

Another musician to take Vodou to the masses was Azor (Leonard Fortune). Born into a family rooted in Vodou, Azor's music reached across boundaries: across nations, across beliefs, across musical styles. He was a musician's musician. His music is filled with Vodou imagery and rhythms. Azor's music is reaching a new audience of ears, eager for fresh sounds and open to the magic that is inherent in Vodou rhythms.

But music is not the only export, nor is it the most important one. The greatest export of Vodou today is art. Sequin flags known as drapo, pounded iron sculptures and electric colored paintings are just some of the major artistic exports coming out of Haiti today. Google the words "Haitian art" and the more than a million hits will give you a brief picture of just how big the market is for Haitian art. People like director Jonathan Demme and writer Edwidge Dandicat have opened the worlds' eyes to the words and artwork of Haiti.

Haitian art is particularly important to Vodou, because although the liturgy is not written down, it is often painted or embroidered upon the artwork that decorates all Vodou temples. For a faith with no real catechism, no Bible or pope, Vodou flags, bottles and paintings often carry great mythic information for those with the eyes to see what is often hidden in plain sight. One of the major artists who gave us this legacy of visuals was Hector Hyppolite, (1894-1948).

A third-generation houngan and a self-taught artist, Hyppolite painted with brushes made of chicken feathers and furniture enamel paints. Using vibrant hues, bold strokes and original themes, Hyppolite painted detailed portraits of island life. But he also had an eye for the spirit world. He painted the Lwa doing many daily tasks – farming, tending animals, cooking

Hyppolite had a knack for portraying the African traditions that infused the island in his paintings. Men plowed fields, women sat in marketplaces. Even the Lwa participated in daily activities like leading animals to pasture and washing clothes. His art caught the attention of painters from other countries. One could make the argument that the Lwa were finding a way to move out into the world through their priest's art.

In the last year of the artist's life, he painted a darker side of Vodou. Subjects included bokors (non-initiated priests said to work with both hands) leading zombies to fields at midnight, snakes winding sinisterly around children and fantastical creatures out of his imagination. He was no longer actively practicing as a houngan, although his home was filled with animistic altars and magical paraphernalia. He claimed, "I asked the spirits' permission to suspend my work...because of my painting... I've always been a priest, just like my father and grandfather, but now I'm more an artist than a priest.[6]" Hyppolite died in the summer of 1948 of a heart attack, leaving behind an amazing collection of art numbered in the hundreds. We have Hyppolite to thank for helping us to see the Lwa in every day scenes, a reminder that we are not alone, but are accompanied by an extraordinary group of Spirits, willing and able to help us even as we hang out the laundry.

When asked why the Lwa looked as they did, Hyppolite said the Lwa themselves told him what they looked like, and how they wished to be represented. As a Mambo who makes Vodou art, I can say most definitely that the spirits of Vodou are very particular about their appearances.

One only has to witness the elaborate toilet of Erzulie Freda to know that the Maitresse loves perfume, but only Anais-Anais; lipstick in just the right shade of rose; and scarves of pink and white. Legba loves walking sticks. Ogoun prefers blue/red mushoirs. The list goes on and on, with each spirit wanting just the right accoutrement for their appearance.

I too, have also worked long hours into the night to get a piece of artwork for the Lwa just right. The Lwa are demanding in their appearance, fussy about the details, and more than willing to tell you (repeatedly) what they look like, what they want and how to do it. There is no need to improvise – the Lwa will tell you right out it is wrong and do it this way!

[6] Rodman, S. (1998). *Where Art is Joy*, New York, NY:Rules de Latour.

The next person to bring the cult of the Lwa to public notice was Andre Pierre. Pierre was born around 1916 in Port-au-Prince. He was a farmer and an active Vodou practitioner. He was introduced to the Centre d'Art in the late 1940's film-maker Maya Deren, who had admired his temple wall paintings. Pierre eventually became a Vodou priest internationally noted for his highly respected visualizations of the Vodou Lwa. Pierre was a LaPlas (the second in command of a Vodou temple) to many people making their kanzos in Haiti, including my own Mama Shakmah, who initiated with him in the late 1960s.

Pierre's work differed from Hyppolite's only in that his Lwa portraits were often placed in highly stylized backgrounds. But the Lwa look remarkably like Hyppolite's – dressed in colonial finery, with many details and ornamentation on their bodies. The colors are electric – with trees often looking as if they were lit from within with high voltage bulbs. The Lwa stare out defiantly at the viewer, as if to say "Look at me! I am beautiful, powerful, royal and unique." Pierre's compositions are highly charged with energy and motion, the spirits vibrantly alive. Through his work, we can travel back in time to see just how glorious the Lwa are. But all great journeys have their end. The lively spirits of Vodou called their painterly priest home to Ginen in October of 2005.

These painters demonstrate a very special point. The Lwa are living, sentient beings. The imagery of the Lwa, down through the years, proves this point dramatically. Whether it has been painted in oils, stitched in sequins or banged out of an oil drum, the look and color of the spirits is consistent and remarkably stable. Artist after artist, without fail, has represented the Lwa as beautiful, vibrant, alive and well appointed. The men are always in dress uniforms, with many decorations and embellishments to their clothing. The ladies are always swathed in voluminous dresses, with hats and accoutrements befitting a royal court. They work in forests lit with an unearthly light. And they are always staring directly at the viewer, as if daring you to see them.

I personally believe the art of a society reveals its inner workings, secrets and moral aesthetics. Through the talented hands of the priestly painters of Vodou, a world of mystery is revealed to those with the eyes to see it.

In a Vodou painting, we are witness to an extraordinary realm of beings, busy at work, thriving at their tasks and doing so in beautifully appointed clothing, without so much as breaking a sweat. The ground lights up where they walk, the trees come alive in gorgeous, unearthly colors and the world around them becomes enlivened in ways we still do not understand. And they call out to be known. They choose artists to paint their pictures, so they can be seen by us. They obviously hunger for communication with us, to such an extent that they inspire artists to paint them looking out into our world.

I want to get to know these folks!

Chapter Four: The Role of Vodou in Haiti

I have talked about the history of Haiti and the inspiration of Vodou to the people. I have told you how the Lwa are desirous of communication with us. Perhaps, all this was in reaction to the conditions that Haitians then and even now find themselves. Surviving in Haiti means each day is a challenge to accomplish even the smallest things. And the time following the revolution was no less arduous than it is today.

After the wars for independence, the country didn't reunify itself. In fact, most books leave out this next part. When the British finally departed from the island, and Dessalines proclaimed Haiti the first black republic of the new World, he was left with no choice but to put the system of slavery right back into place. The only change was in who ruled whom. The mulatto class was not about to be subjugated, having fought so hard to regain what they regarded as their birth right. And there was the issue of foreign aid and debt that needed to be addressed. Haiti could not go back to what it had been, but it needed a monetary base on which to begin something new.

Dessalines understood that in order to move the fledgling country forward, they would have to go back to sugar, to the only agriculture they had ever known. The lighter skin Haitians took over from their foreign masters, and reinstituted the plantation culture. Things were a little better – the cruelties of the white masters were too fresh in the minds of the entire country. But a taste of freedom can change a person. Released from bondage, the men and women of revolutionary Haiti were not ready to go back into servitude. It would take another year of infighting, threats and cruelty to bring people back to the very plantations they had worked so hard to escape off. And it was a cruel irony that many plantations replaced white masters with Haitians.

The new government was not entirely without sympathy to the situation it found itself in. Plots of land were given to those who did not wish to continue on the plantations and were looking to go up into the mountains, perhaps to join family members who had escaped before the revolution. In other places, the people stayed behind – particularly the old and the infirm, who could not make the arduous journey up country. And yet, after all this, there was one more hurdle to overcome.

The revolution that gave freedom to the thousands of slaves had also destroyed the very land they could work on. Millions of acres of plantations and farms had been burned to the ground during the fighting. Wells had been poisoned, rivers damned and diverted, harbors blocked with fish kills by the thousands. Haiti, land of black soil, lush agriculture and verdant yields, was a pitiful shadow of itself. There would be a space of time before food could be grown and crops planted. Now, they would have to wait until the consequences of their actions had bled away, like the top soil of the ground. The plantation culture would continue, but the price would be horrific.

The population became divided – between the ruling mulatto classes and the African slaves. This simple but decidedly self-defeating plan left Haiti with no middle class of people. The slaves only knew how to grow food and survive. They hadn't the education of the enfranchise, nor did they have the means to get one. They had to continue on as best they could.

With no middle class, there was no infrastructure put into place. There were many years of self proclaimed "Emperors," "Kings" and other potentates, all of whom abused the system as badly as and some times worse than the white masters. Money was thrown away on expansive building projects; lavish lifestyles that were imitations of their European counterparts and expensive trips to Europe. With no real agriculture, there was also the import of rare foods and wines to satisfy the ever growing community of *affranchise* who now saw themselves as the upper class of the island population.

This separation of class was to have a devastating effect on the economy of the island. That is because as the affranchise class became smaller and smaller, unwilling to expand their world view into the rest of the country, the peasant classes grew. Land grabbing became very common. Brothers went to war with one another to gain a few acres. It seems that when there is little land, the desire for it is out of proportion to the availability.

In "The Meaning of Africa in Haitian Vodou," Serge LaRose has done an amazing job of recounting the way land was acquired after the revolution[7]. But by his account, one man could easily end up with all the land within a family. This is when we find the beginnings of the Bizango, Sanpwel and Zobop societies. Magical as well as religious in origin, they are also the local law of the mountain people. They hold the land arrangements in long memory, and are called upon to settle land disputes, hereditary claims and death allotments[8]. They are the original Vodou groups, descending from the maroon (runaway) slaves in the mountains. When the local law cannot provide for the people, they can turn once again to Vodou for help when there is no other means of doing something.

Today there are many people living in small rural villages in the interior of the country. The majority of people live clustered in small seaside towns, trying to get along with one another. With no infrastructure, it can make for an odoriferous experience. No regulations means no regular trash collection, no underground sewers. No one regulates slaughter houses and animal markets or their run-off. The country is in the 21st century, but is decidedly back in the 1800s for its internal workings.

---

[7] LaRose, S. "The Meaning of Africa in Haitian Vodou" in *In Symbols and Sentiments: Cross-Cultural Studies in Symbolism.* ed. I.M. Lewis (London:Academic Press, 1977)
[8]*http://web.me.com/yagentanwe/_vodou_ha%C3%AFtien/Bizango_Makaya .html, accessed 01/14/10*

If you are a poor mother with kids, this lifestyle can be devastating. But if you belong to a Vodou sosyete, then you can sleep beneath its protective tonnel (the roof over the dance floor.) The mambo will share whatever meager resources she has with her "ti-fey", the little leaves of the sosyete -- a reference to the many children she has made through initiation. This is why I am asked all the time "how many children do you have?" They are not talking about children of my body, but rather children of my soul. Children, be they blood or spiritual mean support, safety and security - all rare commodities in a place like Haiti. Let's say your kids need clothes for school. You can appeal to the Mambo, and she will provide. Or if you are sick, or one of your kids becomes ill, the Mambo will try to cure you, and if she can't then, she will send you to the doctor, and pay for the visit herself. She can do this, because Vodou is a paid priesthood. Through rituals, baths, readings, services such as Sevis or Kanzo, the Mambo raises money to take care of herself, her family and her house. In a country where there are no social services, Vodou provides much needed medical, welfare and moral services.

Larger, more well-off Vodou houses make a very big deal out of their position. They often do big public fets, where food and drink is abundant. Our kanzo was attended by hundreds of folks from the neighborhood. They knew that the Mambo was providing meat and rice, and that at least for one night, there'd be food, music and dancing. Sometimes, for special services, the people might get a little money for helping out. After all, there is wood to collect for the fire, laundry to be done, water to gotten, floors to be swept, mats to put away. There is always something that needs to be done. A Vodou dance is a way for the local community to come together to enjoy a meal, have camaraderie and make a few coins for the week.

Membership in a Vodou house makes you a part of the community. With time and effort, you move into the role of hounsi, and finally, you may begin to work your way toward kanzo. With the advent of non-Haitians coming down to Haiti, there is also the chance of making new friends and possibly getting out of the confines of a restrictive country, where many folks are hemmed in by the daily struggle to survive.

When we were in Saut d'Eau in 2008, I was surprised at the English I heard spoken, and the erudite manners of the folks we met along the road. Of course, Saut d'Eau is one of the biggest festivals in all of Haiti and tens of thousands of folks descend upon the tiny village to part take of Danbala's pools and Erzulie's blessings. That includes Haitians as well as foreigners. Little Saut d'Eau has found its place in the world and the inhabitants of the village know it. They encounter Americans, Brits and Austrians – the world as a matter of fact. The young man who accompanied me down to the falls asked if I knew So-and-So, his good friend from Germany. I politely said no, but maybe I would meet him sometime. My young guide nodded, answering that when he saw his German friend again, he would tell him about me. I said thank you and we continued our walk in silence as his world expanded by knowing a photographer in Germany and now an American mambo. Vodou had brought another piece of the world to his doorstep. Not through a newspaper, not through a TV show – through a person on the path to the waterfalls, an American walking with her friends. Vodou includes, it does not exclude.

I am forever amazed by the events and people that Vodou brings together. The Vodou spirits reach out through time and space, connecting people, making friends of strangers, families out of people who have no connection to one another other than their interest in Vodou. We were staying at the Hotel Oloffson, surely the main crossroads in all of Port au Prince. We had only been in the country 22 hours, when a smiling Ti-Jean Michael of the Marche Fer (the Vodou Iron Market) made his arrival on the patio of the hotel. He strolled up to me with a big smile and asked if I was Mambo Pat. I said yes, how did he know I was here? He never missed a beat – answering that his good friend Grete told him and that he had been waiting for me. I knew Grete only via a single phone call, made before I had come down to Haiti. But the Lwa reach out beyond time and space, connecting Ti-Jean and I. I gave Ti-Jean my shopping list and said I'd be back in couple of days, would he mind taking care of it for me? He smiled and answered "*Pa pwoblem.*" Without fail, four huge bags awaited me at the hotel upon my return. Ti-Jean had kept his word and done all my shopping for the price he named. Would you hand a total stranger $300 in America and think you'd find your stuff four days later? This could happen only in Haiti, where strangers connect in ways that we can only begin to imagine.

Vodou provides safety, security, support. But Vodou's biggest role today is to provide a religious practice that reflects back all the ingenuity, creativity and faith that its practitioners bring to it. The Vodou religion is all about the people of Haiti. The island is said to be 90% Catholic and 100% Vodou. But try as they may, the religions of the book can't take away the need to practice Vodou. It is as much a part of the island as the people themselves.

In a Vodou service, you don't just pray to God, you speak directly to Him through His emissaries the Lwa. And at times, you become one with them. The Lwa descend and take their servitors to places within themselves that are glorious, uplifting and inspiring. Where else can you sit down and talk to the angels face to face? The drums are irresistible, the dance infectious. You become caught up in the energy and it is on purpose. A Vodou service is a community of practitioners who work together – hard – to offer up their pain and receive blessings with abandon.

Vodou liturgy is sung in a style called Call and Response. It is a conversation between the choir, the song master and the drums. It is a three way dialog about life, love, work, family, and much, much more. A well done ritual is a production as lavish as anything on Broadway. The stage is set with brilliant white clothing, swirling flags and sweeping movements, all of which centers on the poto mitan, the center post of the lakou. All the movement is designed to bring the Lwa down to this plane of existence, so They may speak to the congregation.

Dances of Vodou also reflect the African populations that brought them to the island: The supple movements of the royal Yanvalou, the upright defiance of a Petro step. The collective inclusiveness of the Djouba or Ibo dances. All is a reflection of the many styles of African nations who gave their gifts of body and voice to the faith of Vodou.

Even temples reflect their African origins. The Rada altar is a stepped affair of many layers, glittering with sequins and glass, draped in white cloths that harkens to its royal antecedents. Those antecedents speak back to the ancestors of African origin who are served through the color white, a symbol of their purity and power. Petro altars are violent, red, angry bricolage that display the island side of slavery, with chains, whistles and whips as part of the display. And these visual arts are further refracted as they embodied the many styles of nations and subsets of people – Ibo, Djoubas, Senegal and Kapalou.

Depending on where the temple is located, the very ground becomes a sanctuary that speaks to Africa. The giant Mapou trees of Souvenance are ancestral vehicles of spirit, possibly having been brought here from Africa during the Middle Passage. Their seed pods might have been used as food for the Africans held as slaves in the ship. Or the pod was on the branches that might have been cut and used as bedding. We have no idea how they arrived, but we do know they are not native to Haiti. The Artibonite river is home to many Lwa and spirits for those who settled its banks. And anyone who has gone to the glorious falls of Saut d'Eau (where the Virgin Mary is said to have appeared) or historic Plaine Nord (site of the first revolutionary battle for freedom) can speak of the energy in those natural places. They pulse with spiritual electricity, sending shivers up your arms and standing your hair on end. The very ground you walk on is filled with the bodies and blood of those who went before you. In Haiti, one really does stand on the shoulders of those who died.

In all these places, there are families living and working, who owe a part of their existence to their inclusion in a Vodou house. I saw this in the ironworkers village of Croix de Bouquets. Here artists give voice and meaning to the spirits of Vodou through steel and hammers. The ringing of those hammers and the laughter of children mix with a hum that you can hear from the roadway. As I wandered among the artist's shops, an unassuming doorway beckoned. The man standing by the door saw me looking at the streamers dangling from the interior ceiling and invited me to step into the room behind. It was a peristyle, simply appointed and delightfully shaded from the heat of the sun. The ceiling was festooned with strings of paper streamers, the poto mitan painted with serpentine designs and the walls decorated with images of the Lwa in their Catholic finery – Ogoun riding his white stallion as Saint Jacques Major, Mambo Ayizan meditating over the chalice as Saint Claire.

I kissed the poto mitan upon entering. The houngan who had invited me in to the peristyle watched, nodding in approval.

"You are mambo?" he asked.

"Yes," I replied.

"Where is your peristyle?" he said.

"In the USA."

He stood silently in thought for a moment, studying my face. Nodding again, he said, "Then the Lwa must be pleased that you are here." Once again, Vodou had included even me, a *blan* on a dusty little pathway in Croix de Mission.

Chapter Five: Basic Theology

Vodou is a complex faith that gives the casual viewer a glimpse into a fantastic universe of spirit. The faithful gain entry by dancing, singing and giving over their bodies to the Lwa. The gifts the Spirits confer are healing and balance in life. So how does one gain permission to enter this realm of light and healing? Through the theology of Vodou, also known as the Reglemen.

When talking about Vodou, there are many paths to understanding its complex nature. We have to remember that the Africans who came to the island via the Middle Passage were comprised of many different nations of people: Kongo, Ibo, Senegal, Alarada, Nago. They didn't speak one another's languages much less know each other's religions. These people were intelligent, educated and skilled members of their societies. They were farmers, herdsmen, weavers, herbalists, military strategists, midwives and ironsmiths.

There are multiple ways in which these nations of people evolved and developed their faith. Into this mix of people, we have to add the diverse number of theologies, spirits, dances, songs, musical styles and drum rhythms that each nation of people held as their personal view of how to speak with the Divine. As you travel across the island of Haiti, you find that each area has its own unique set of religious practices, songs, drum rhythms and dances, reflecting the multi-dimensional nature of the Lwa and the Africans who remembered them.

Let me begin with the Kongo nation, which heavily influenced the theology of Haitian Vodou. The Kongo nation provided what has been said to be the largest portion of slave population to the island of Haiti[9]. Nearly half of all the Africans brought to the island were Kongolese. Records showed slave ships arriving in Port-au-Prince from Africa carried far more Kongolese people than any other.

The Kongo people had very sophisticated view of the world. They saw it has having four distinct and separate parts equalling or mirroring the four movements of sun, which in turn mirrored the four paths of man. One begins at sunrise, signifying a physical birth into the world and heralding a new beginning. Then, there is growth, where a person accumulates knowledge and experience through life. This is similar to Noon, when the sun is high in the sky and all the earth grows and flourishes under its rays. A person's physical death is like the end of the day, when the sun sets. And finally, a person is time of rest is accorded the sun at midnight. This is the time in which the soul returns to the underworld, similar to that of the Egyptians or the Sumerians. In the Vodou faith, we call it *Anba Dlo* or Under the Waters. It is a time of rest, recuperation and reflection.

---

[9] Lovejoy, P. (2000). *Transformation in Slavery*. New York: Cambridge University Press.

The Kongolese divided these four segments into two distinct areas: one for the living and one for the dead. The living move freely on this plane of existence. And the dead move within a large body of water called Kalunga. Two planes of existence, each with its own rules and reasons for separation would cause untold calamity if crossed or intersected in any way.

There is also an entire body of religious practice – that of propitiation – that is based on the idea of keeping the worlds of men and gods separate. To propitiate the Gods, they are given an offering, so they stay in their own world, and leave this one alone.

I have a visual idea of the first time the world of the Africans was breached by something that was not of their own plane of existence. This is my own interpretation. There are no records, so I can only surmise what the Kongo people may have thought when they saw the great white sails of the Portuguese ships on the horizon at the Bight of Benin. White is the color of the ancestors in Africa, and huge white sails could have meant the dead were approaching land. This would have been further interpreted as death by the sight of the white skinned Portuguese sailors. As propitiation was the practice, the king would have offered the best thing he had at the time, to make the "dead" go away – prisoners from the great wars that were being waged at that time.

The Atlantic crossing might have been interpreted as the Kalunga for the African prisoners. The Middle Passage, as the trip across the Atlantic Ocean became known, would have felt like death, since so many Africans died during that passage. And this idea of the dead residing in the waters has remained to this day within the theology of Vodou.

Upon arriving in the New World, the Africans were separated from one another. Plantation owners would deliberately not place people of the same nation together. This was based on the idea that separating the nations of Africans would help control them. When you consider the diversity of people the Africans became mixed in with – Spanish, French, and Native, it begins to make sense that the finer points of the Kongo theology became displaced with other ideas and paradigms.

Over time, the Kalunga evolved into the Abysmal Waters, where the dead of Vodou reside, awaiting their rebirth here on Earth or their entrance to Ginen. The same passage over water that took them away from Africa would become the waters of return that had to be crossed in order to get back to the homeland.

The island itself also contributed to the religious mix. Rachel Beauvoir-Dominique has written extensively on the contributions of the Amerindians who were still on the island at the very beginning of the plantation culture. She makes a compelling argument that the maroon slaves joined with the natives, and brought the Indians' guerrilla tactics, intimate knowledge of the landscape and their night time stealth to their fight for independence[10]. Even the Tainos left behind the maraca and the possibly the concept of Papa Loko as a vegetation Lwa. All this is just another way of saying that many types of religious practices were seamlessly blended into a whole that we have come to know as Haitian Vodou.

Other African nations also contributed to the theological bricolage of Vodou. The Ibo contributed their own religious ideas, beginning with the concept of a creator who is distant and uncaring about the world, but who has left behind a cadre of spirits. The govis (receptacle jars for the Lwa), canaries (receptacle jars for the dead) and pot tets (receptacle jars for initiates) find their origin in the Ibo's use of pots as vessels for their gods.[11] The Nago of West Africa lent their military stratagems and organization to the Rara parades of today. The military prowess of the Nago nation is legendary. Some scholars point to the success of the Battle of Veritieres as being won by a strong Nago force in the African army.

The Nago nation has an over arching influence on most things in Haiti. Coming from old Dahomey, which today we call Benin, the red, blue and gold of the Nago nation permeates all the Petro aspects of Vodou. The colors are the dominant ones for Petro Lwa such as Ogoun and Dantor. The military Lwa such as the

---

[10] Beauvoir-Dominique, R. (2007). The vodou-makaya artistic tradition in haiti's heritage. In Mathez, P. & Hainard, J. (Ed.), *Vodou: A Way of Life* (pp. 167-174). Genève: Infolio/Musée d'ethnographie de Genèva
[11] Basden, G. T. (2008). *Among the Ibos of Nigeria*. Ann Arbor, MI: UMI Microform 3297540.

Ogouns, some of the Simbis in the south and even the Bossous of the north, are all seen as having a military face. They arrive in service with the strutting posture of a military parade marshal. They call for their uniforms and swords, braids and *agwesans*, the cross chest banners of red and blue ribbons with large gaudy rosettes at the hips. They march around the temple, saluting and bellowing orders. And they are very proud of their military record, bragging long and loudly into the night of their achievements.

In terms of religious influence, we see the Nago nation in the style of seating for a ceremony, with the most important dignitaries up front, and the rows receding back in order of bearing/importance. In our own temple, the Asogwe ranks sit up close to the altar. Behind them are seated the Su Pwens, and behind them the Hounsis. The bossales (non-initiated) and visitors are left to smaller sections. This seating by rank and file is dominant in most of temples I have visited.

Recently, we participated in a local Fet Guédé. The presiding Mambos and Houngans all huddled up close to the altar, enclosing it as they sang through the Priye Ginen. The invited visitors (this included us) were lined up behind them. The rest of the group was seated off to one side. Position was everything -- the locals rearranged and reseated themselves until a satisfactory order was established.

This order of seating is prevalent in all areas of Haiti. It is most often an implied ordering, although at times it is quite public, as in the ranks and roles of a Rara carnival band. This is the most public demonstration of Nago influence.

Rara, those country carnival bands that seem to appear out of nowhere and march up along roadsides and pathways are ubiquitous all throughout Haiti during the Lenten season. Comprised of drummers, horn players and blowers of the amazing vaccines, the large bamboo tubes that produce a single note, they walk at night throughout the countryside. They are entertained at various lakous, where they can camp for the evening, resting and in the morning, receive money and food for their performance. Liza McAlister has done an amazing job of writing about Rara and her web site[12] is a wealth of knowledge. McAlister makes some points about Rara that are pertinent to our discussion about Nago.

Rara bands are referred to as "armies." They are led by Generals, Majors (*major jonc*) and lieutenants, who determine the routes and the stops along their walk-about. When two bands or "armies" meet at a crossroads, they stage a mock battle with one another, punctuated by singing, drumming and dancing. Each "army" attempts to outdo the other, with elaborate rhythms, wildly suggestive lyrics and complicated dance steps. When a satisfactory ending has been reached, they share swigs of *kleren* (raw cane liquor) and move along into the night. These mock confrontations further illustrate the military influence of the Nagos.

---

[12] *http://rara.wesleyan.edu/index.php, Liza McAllister*

And finally, one of the biggest Nago festivals is held each year on July 24 and 25th at the intersection of a simple country road in Plaine Nord or the Northern Plains, just outside of the city of Cap Haitian. This location is important because of its historic role in the Haitian revolution.

The northern plains were among the most fertile of the plantations. They were also the most isolated. The plantation owners in this area wanted autonomy from the rest of the country, so they could do as they pleased. They thought their slave populations would not revolt, due to their isolation from the southern plantation slaves. They were wrong.

On the night of August 22, 1791, the largest slave uprising to occur in Haiti plunged the country into civil war. Thousands of Africans in the north region rose up to take vengeance on their masters and to fight for liberty. Within ten days, they had taken control of the entire Northern Province in an unprecedented revolt that led the eventual independence of the island. This was the beginning of the Haitian Revolution[13]. And for this reason, the crossroads at Plaine Nord is dedicated to Papa Ogoun, fierce Nago warrior who inspired the African slaves to fight for their rights and their freedoms and is revered as the patron of the Revolution.

Today, the mud hole is less a historical site than a religious one. For most of the year the town is a sleepy village but on July

---

[13] Rogozinski, Jan (1999). *A Brief History of the Caribbean (Revised ed.).* New York: Facts on File, Inc

23rd, the population swells to three times its usual number. *Marchands* (market women) set up shop along the dirt street that leads to a sink hole that could swallow a school bus. This hole is fed by an underground spring, and creates a wallow that is soon filled with offerings of flesh both living and divine, as well as bottles of Barbanncourt, perfume and anything being offered as a gift to Papa Ogoun during the festival. The mud is thought to have curative powers, so women bathe their children in it, old men seek virility in its gooey depths and everyone attributes miraculous power to its viscous coating.

The Nago nation's influence is also seen in the use of sequin flags in the temple proper. Tina Girouard's landmark book, *Sequin Artists of Haiti*, details these amazing flags, their ritual uses and their inclusion in both Vodou ceremonies as well as the costumes of the Rara groups. Borrowed from the military parades of the Nago, the flags have both a liturgical purpose as well as a non-spiritual life as works of art.

In service, the flags are used to indicate the major Lwa served by a given house. The most important Lwa are fetted with the most elaborate flags the houmfort can afford. Older flags were more military in style, favoring satin cloth and elaborate fringe, over heavy embellishment. Today, sequin flags or *drapo*, are one of Haiti's most ubiquitous exports.

Even the bearers of the flags have military roles. In a Vodou temple, they are generally carried by a woman, and she is named the *Reine Drapo* or Flag Queen. In Rara, the flags are held by the lieutenants for the *Major Jonc* or leader and signal the watching crowd as to which Lwa walks with the Rara parade.

Flags are not used in all temples. Whether it is due to the ubiquitous nature of the flag as an exported art piece, or the cost has become too great, the twirling flourish of flags has become one of the elements of a service that has dropped off. Honorable and venerable houngans, such as Ayti Max Beauvoir, still deploy them at the start of their services. My own Papa Edgar Jean-Louis also used flags for his most important services, such as a kanzo or Three Kings Day. But these are rare instances when these flags are brought forth for public viewing. I believe that the flags have decreased in popularity due to Vodou fets becoming less of a religious observance and more of an excuse for people to party. A friend in Miami says that she has abandoned the services and fets in her area, due to the disrespectful attitude of the younger generation. "They seem to view a Vodou fet as an excuse – to drink, to act out and to be disrespectful to the elders," she has said. "They no longer remember why we do this."

As the faith moves out into non-Haitian communities, the formalities associated with it are becoming consigned to the side lines. Space may also play a part, as temples in the Diaspora are often much smaller than their Haitian counter parts.

The third contributor to the theological bricolage of Vodou is the Dahomean influence. From the Dahomeans we receive the many names of the Lwa and their various groupings or escorts.

The chart below is just a small sample of the many names that still correlate to their African roots:

African Name	Haitian name
Agasu	Agassou
Aizen	Ayizan
Dangbe Ayido Hwedo	Danbala Aida Wedo
Gu	Ogoun
Guede	Guédé
Hevioso	Sobo/Bade/Agarou
Agwe	Agwe Tawayo
Legba	Atibon Legba
Tohonsu	Bossou

Some names stayed nearly identical – such as Legba -- while others changed into not just one name but three, as in the split of Hevioso to Sobo, Bade and Agarou. This remembering of names, personalities and proto-types was all done under the most extreme conditions. The fact that anyone remembered anything at all is a miracle. The re-naming of spirits was one way in which the religion blended for all the nations of Africans who found themselves united in misery under a common enemy – the plantation masters.

Dahomey was the old name of Benin, and was an important coastal city-state. Three powerful clans ruled here from the mid 1600s to the late 1800s. It was also an important slave center, because many ships found their prisoners at its port. Many nations of people were brought to Dahomey for sale to the slave ships bound for the new world. There are records of the king of Dahomey telling the slaves they would be shipped out but not forgotten. They were allowed a short time to say goodbye to their homeland. There are records of the very sad and poignant farewells written by the Africans themselves. These stories speak to the pain and pathos of these people leaving their homes.

This variety of nations, rhythms, songs and spirits, as well as the emotional content of those songs, gave rise to the intricate world of Vodou that we know of today. Although a Vodou ceremony may seem like a complex and contrary affair, filled with drum beats, iron bells and voices singing against their rhythms, it is in fact, an orderly and highly evolved system of communing with the Divine, remembering where people came from and the hope that tomorrow will bring an end to the suffering.

To begin to unravel the secrets of Vodou, we have to remember that all rituals evolve to reflect the societies that give rise to them. Vodou is no different.

The world of the African slave was a hard and cruel one. Work was relentless, rest elusive and hunger a constant companion. When given the rare day off, the Africans didn't just sit around. They had to grow food to eat, make or repair clothing, tend to their sick. They also found time to sing, drum, and to remember. They repeatedly recollected who they were, where they came from and when they might one day return to that place. They used this hope, this energy of remembering to order their rituals, so that they would find a way to go back to that promised land of memory.

Vodou is a faith of remembrance. The enslaved nations used what we know as a mnemonic device to create the world they left behind. It was not the real Africa, but one of embellished memory and fond recall. They were building a place that did not exist physically except in their minds.

They began by giving the memory a name – Ginen, a mythical land where they all originated from. It did not matter what nation they were from, they had all arrived the same way: on a great sailing ship over a vast and dark expanse of water. And their spirits came this way as well, riding in the heads of their servitors. This is one possible explanation for the head being so important in Vodou. The head became the physical adytum of the Lwa – the Temple not made with hands.

The dark expanse of water they had crossed became the Water Road back to Ginen, land of myth and memory. In services, the Africans would sing and dance themselves back to that place. They made offerings not to chase the Lwa away, but to bring them here, to this time and this place, so that the Africans could ask for advice, healing, blessings. When they had nothing to offer for thanks or for propitiation, they would always have water – the very sweat of their bodies would be enough to offer up to the spirits.

And so today, we have the water road of Vodou. All ceremonies begin by pouring water on the floor of the temple, to aid the spirits in their arrival. It is an allusion to the water road of the Atlantic crossing that brought the Africans to the New World, the same water road that some of the slaves drowned in, rather than be taken against their will to a strange place. We share some of this history, through the story of the Flying Africans at Dunbar Creek in Georgia[14]. There are two stories about the Africans. One is the "white" version, where the Ibos broke free and walked into Dunbar Creek, choosing to drown rather than remain enslaved. And the "black" version, where one morning, the plantation manager goes to the fields looking for the Ibos who refused to working as chattel. As the manager approached them, they rose up into the sky, turned into buzzards and flew back to Africa. Whatever happened, we remember these brave men and women who chose to leave this plane of existence rather than submit to chattel and bondage. They too, took the water road back to Ginen.

The water Road of Ginen is also the road of our own bodies, the blood and sweat of our selves, offered up as a vessel for spirit to come down and enter. All three scenarios – the mythical road of water across the Atlantic Ocean, the Water Road of the Temple and the Water of the Body -- are relevant to the practice of the Vodou faith.

---

[14] *http://www.georgiaencyclopedia.org/nge/Article.jsp?id=h-2895, accesed 8/7/10*

Water is the central element of a service. It is poured out for the Lwa to walk on. It is offered up as a gift for the Divine to bless. It is poured over the congregation as a unifying gesture of both cleansing and comfort. Water and all the attending symbologies of water – intuition, dreams and emotions – come into play when water is used in ritual.

We consecrate and bless a large pan or kivet of water prior to service, so that the spirits will find it pleasing and come forth. We wash everyone's hands with this consecrated water before service, to unify us, cleanse us and bring us together in focus and intent. We use this same water to open a service by pouring water in all four quarters, thereby allowing the spiritual forces to align properly. Like the ocean that brought the Africans to the new world, we use water to bring ourselves back to the place of memory and myth within ourselves. We let the water connect us to a higher potential, a higher source. By doing so, we find peace and balance within ourselves, so that we can maintain our equilibrium outside of ourselves.

The intent of a Vodou ritual is to bring us back across the mythical waters of return, the abysmal waters or however one chooses to think of it. It returns us to the land of our Ancestors, where we will find great knowledge, comfort and answers to our questions. This place was called "Ginen" by the slaves and we still use that name today. It is a mythical place of pure memory that serves as the guiding principle in our lives.

How is it that I, an American, can return to this place that was the root of so many Africans? I return because it is a place for everyone. My papa Kanzo Fritzner Georges told me that Ginen is where everyone came from and everyone has a place there. As he has since died and returned to Ginen, I keep his words alive by believing in the truth of them. I believed Papa Fritzner when he told me that Ginen was big enough for us all. One day, I know I too, will return there to the place where my fathers wait for me.

And in support of that belief, we metaphorically return to Ginen at the beginning of each service we hold. We achieve this metaphysical passage by reciting a magical incantation, a poem, a prayer. This recitation is the key to opening the veil between here and Ginen. It employs a very old standard of memory work. By reciting where we came from, we can return by the same way. This recitation is known today as the Priye Ginen.

The Priye Ginen or Prayer of Africa is a long mnemonic device used to facilitate a state of grace for the participants. Ordered specifically for each house, it is the manner in which all the differing nations of Africans were able to come together and work as one in the face of such awful conditions.

The Priye orders the entire work of a Vodou service. It states unequivocally who we are, where we came from and where we are going. To fully appreciate its beauty, you need only listen to a group of priests as they sing their way through a Priye. The structure of the prayer is like a set of nesting bowls, one seated within another, layer upon layer.

The Priye Ginen opens with the Priye Litany. This portion starts with Catholic hymns. There are old French canticles, modern Catholic songs and repetitive passages meant to create a connection between the saints and the congregation. Although the stanzas vary somewhat from house to house, the majority of these hymns are identical in all houses. They are sung to demonstrate a return to the origin of mankind.

The beginning of the prayer is always in French. That was the language on the island of Haiti, way back at the start of the plantation culture and up to this very day. It was the language of the masters, learned via the Catholic Church's catechism and enforced visits to mass on Sunday. The Africans would learn it, as it would become the common thread for them all. They would make it their own, blending French words with African syntax structure. And they would keep the verses that spoke most plainly to their own conditions. Some examples are:

"Vene Bon Dieu, Vene a moi" – "Come my sweet God, come to me," an imploring request to find the Divine both in the physical place of Haiti, as well as in themselves.

"Vous qui vive, dans la souffrance..." – "You who have lived in suffering..." A statement of fact given the lives of the Africans in that time frame.

The second part of the Priye is called the Priye Djo and it refers to the call and response listing of the saints, Lwa and the ancestral lineage that the sosyete worships, serves and remembers.

This section of the Priye is sung in Creole, a reminder to us all that this is the portion that unites us as brothers and sisters. These are the common ancestors we all share: Ogoun the warrior, who is every military man or woman we have ever known; Erzulie Freda, the loving mother figure; Azaka the farmer, who represents all the hard working people of the world; Guédé the unruly clown of death who reminds us all that in the end, we are all dust. Within this listing are the archetypes of the world, set out as spirits whose experiences and personalities we can see in our own lives.

These spirits are the legacy of the extraordinary men and women who created the Priye Ginen and used it as their guiding principle and light. Set within its many verses (and in some houses, hundreds of verses) are the keys to opening the way between here and Ginen. One merely needs to know how to work the lock, to allow the door to open and the riches of Ginen to tumble forth.

As we sing our way through the Priye Djo, we eventually come to the mysteries of the Africans, who left behind a bevy of clues and hints, hidden in the *langaj* of the Priye.

Langaj are the many words in the Priye that seem to make no sense. They are not French, nor are they Creole. They are something else all together. They are the language of Africa left behind by the enslaved Africans. We use them as words of power and enchantment that were spoken over and over again, but never understood. Three hundred years of recitation, like an extended game of Whisper down the Lane, has left us bereft of their meaning, but not of their power. The *langaj* of the Priye is a rich brew of sounds and accents, meanings and metaphor. Some people are working hard to compile a dictionary of meanings, sussing out the accents, figuring out the nations and what the words mean literally. I am not one them.

I look at them as having a powerful vibratory energy. One doesn't need to know the real meaning, and in fact, it would spoil it for me personally if I did. Speaking them clearly, just as they were spoken, is all that is necessary to use them. I say them as they were said to me, with care. I use them when it is appropriate, as in service. I do not switch one word for another. I use them sincerely and with intent. That they do work is all I need to know. But having them is a fascinating bit of history.

These words, this *langaj*, is all we have left of all those who have gone before us. They were enslaved nations of African men and women who owned nothing. They had no tools to write, no books to leave behind. All they had were their names, their memories and their voices. So they wrote their liturgy in spoken words; they emblazoned their belief with rhythm and they shared what they had learned with one another through singing.

Vodou is an oral tradition due to circumstance and reality. The songs would survive – the old Africans realized this on the crossing. If the songs survived, then the memory of Africa would too. And so they used what they had to create a liturgical body that has endured up to this very day. They used their minds and their hearts to encode the world that they remembered in song. They spoke it to one another weekly, sometimes daily. They created sacred space from nothing, because they carried it within themselves. They repeated their liturgy to one another, until they could remember it from heart. And they changed or added to it as their lives changed, so that it would remain fresh and up to date always. They created an amazing gift for us – a living faith that would continue to evolve with its practitioners, for as long as anyone would need it to do so. And it continues to this very day – living side by side with Haitians, Americans, Canadians and many, many others who have found the ancient power of the Africans.

I am often asked to compare Catholicism and Vodou. My answer is to look at the similarities instead. Like the African Ancestors, I choose not to see the differences, but to celebrate the common links. This chart demonstrates some of those commonalities I spoke about.

Vodou	**Modern Catholicism**
Monotheistic religion	Monotheistic religion
Bon Dye embodies all of creation	One God embodies all of creation
Host of lesser spirits called Lwa / Mysteries	Host of lesser spirits called Saints / Angels
Highly ordered calendar of observances, feast days, and celebrations	Highly structured calendar of holy days, feast days, and observances

Structured, formal rituals celebrated with music and dance	Structured liturgical calendar, celebrated with song and prayers
Hundreds of songs, all passed via oral tradition	Hundreds of songs, written and handed down

The Africans placed within Vodou their own theological view of the Spirit world. I like to say they Africanized Christian elements, to compliment and supplement what was lost to them, via the Middle Passage to the New World.

They adopted prayers, images and the theological ideas that were a mirror of their own spiritual concepts. They may have hidden their own take on the faith, but they certainly did not change their world view to that of a Christian. They were already aware of Christian concepts, due to the zealous spread of Christianity in the Kongo from the Capuchin and other holy orders who had infiltrated the African country side for more than a century. There are many books on the Christianization of the Kongo people, beginning as early as the 1480s. The Hollywood version would have you believe that the Africans were forced into Christianity. The Kongo kings were adherents to the Christian doctrine, but that was only one small part of the African population. The majority of people still worshipped as their forefathers had done. And it is this generational memory which I feel was the catalyst for the Vodou we know today.

The Africans of the colonial era in Haiti choose to line up their faith, their practices and their outward observances with the faith of their masters, because they had no choice. Their lives were so rigidly enforced and ruled, they couldn't break off to propitiate their own deities. So they placed them alongside those of their masters, and served as best they could. The African Spirits adjusted as well. The theological set up is very simple. Please look at this chart below:

GOD
The Mysteries: Lwa, Saints, Angels
Ancestors
Guédé
The Living

Vodou is monotheistic. There is one God, who can be viewed as both Divine Mother and Father. Many people find that to be surprising, because they hear about the numerous Lwa and think they are gods. They are not. We worship God as a creator who embodies male and female sides, but who is without sex or orientation. God simply is and we worship that principle.

Below God are the Lwa. In Haiti, they are referred to simply as the 'Mysteries.' The word 'Lwa' has come to be attached to a more mundane idea of spirits that are here to help us. Lwa is the outer name of the Spirits (just like a person having two names, a public and a private, the Lwa also have public and private names). Public names are the popular ones that everyone knows or uses. Ogoun, Ezili, Gran Bwa. These are the "public" names of the Lwa. But in service, the private names are learned and used. The use of private Lwa names shows that the servitor is in a relationship with the spirit and is not a layperson.

Below the Lwa are the Ancestors, those people who are in your bloodline, have died and are not yet ascended to the status of Lwa. These Ancestors are the real ones, not the invoked ones. And Ancestors are not just the recent dead, meaning the ones you can actually remember living. The word "ancestor" most often refers to the oldest dead in your family bloodline.

Below the Ancestors, we find the guédé (with a small "g"). This class of spirits is the most confusing to people but also the most ubiquitous. The word Guédé means dead, and anyone who has died is a Guédé in the Vodou lexicon. Let's just stay with the overarching concept for now.

And finally, we have the Living who serve all these spirits above them. This is one of the reasons why we say you do not need to find Lwa to serve, nor do you pick the Lwa. They pick you. Think about that for one moment. An Energy, a living Entity that can move through time and space, chooses you to be Their emissary here on Earth. Of all the people on the planet, this incredible spirit chooses to walk with you for as long as you are here on this earth. This Spirit is the most like you, sharing likes and dislikes with you. They are the mirror of you in Heaven, and you are their mirror here on earth. They can move heaven and hell for you, if you wish it to be so. They can open opportunities, inspire you to greatness, motivate you to do things you might not even realize or think about. They choose to do this, both with and for you. Think about that for one moment. And then, think about the stupidity of saying you choose them.

Do not believe the popular press's idea that Vodou is simple or unsophisticated in its theology. The continent of Africa that gave us the slave populations also gave us the highly ordered and complicated faith of the Ancient Egyptians, the ancestrally focused practices of the Sumerians and the star-based theology of the Chaldeans. These same cultures were mapping the skies, creating calendars and predicting earth based phenomenon such as tidal waves and earthquakes before Isaac Newton was even around to dream about gravity and planets.

A star based theology that utilizes the movement of the earth to predict planting seasons. Sophisticated death rituals that recognize and honor a life beyond this mortal one. Ancestral rites that give respect to those who have gone before, so that those who follow can live a better life. All this is found throughout the Vodou religion. To truly appreciate and grasp the complexity of this faith, you must begin by understanding yourself. And that knowledge starts with your soul and its various components.

Ayti Max Beauvoir, honor to him, has written and lectured extensively about the soul in Vodou. Papa Max defines the soul as having five components[15]. They are as follows:

Gro Bon Anj – This is literally the "big good angel" in kreyol. This is the Divine particle in each person, whose job it is to keep each of us alive. It is our very breath of Life, the animating force by which we move and breathe in the world. This is what is captured and turned into a zombie by the bokor, a non-initiated priest of Vodou. When a person dies, it is the Gro Bon Anj that is freed during the rites of Dessounen, the ritual of release for someone who has died.

Ti Bon Anj – This is the "little good angel" in Kreyol. Immortal and indestructible, it is the spiritual principle and intellect of each person. Here is where your seat of Memory and Will resides. It can leave the body at any time – and vacates for intercession by the Lwa. When you die, this is the part that stands before God and recants what it has learned from its time on earth. Together, the Ti Bon Anj and God decide on the next incarnation. The Met Tet stays by the Ti bon Anj for all its incarnations, remembering the conversation and the goals of each life time. As the Ti Bon Anj descends into matter, it consciously forgets what it chose to accomplish. But the Met Tet (your Guardian Angel as it

---

[15] Beauvoir, M. *www.vodou.org*, accessed 1/12/2004

were) remembers and spends the life cycle on earth helping the Ti Bon Anj realize its potential and goals.

Nanm – This is the vital energy residing in every cell of a person. Seat of genetics, this is the part of you that you keep from your ancestors. It is the biological guard of your blood. Your very DNA. The Nanm is the definition of who you are, the sum of all you came from and the potential for all you can be.

Zetwal – is literally your "star", your destiny. A person's zetwal resides outside the body, just as an actual Star does in heaven. Only this star is the metaphysical kind and resides in an ocean of metaphysical stars. It is the guardian of your spiritual calabash, providing what is good for each person's amelioration and spiritual advancement. It is worth mentioning here that this concept comes from the Egyptian belief in the eternal night of the soul. Many existing papyri speak of a person's soul traveling by starlight to the Hall of the Assessors, where the soul is weighed by Ma'at. Her judgment then sends the soul back to earth for another lifetime. As the soul leaves the hall, starlight again guides it back to earth, where it rises to live again. The star is an ever present celestial guide, directing the soul's progress on its earthly voyage. Many Pharonic tombs had their ceilings splattered with five pointed stars. The secret symbol of Egypt was in fact a pentacle, signifying the Solar/Stellar/Sky origin of its Pharaohs. I had worn a circled star to Haiti when I was going through my kanzo. It became the point of countless examinations and requests to touch. I had no idea why then, but now I understand its significance and place in the celestial musings of Vodou.

Lwa Met Tet – literally means the Spirit of your Head. It is the entity that vibrates at your frequency and with whom you have the most in common. You are your Met Tet's face here on earth. They are your face in heaven. In a sense, the manner in which you lead your life gives the Met Tet a chance to elevate Themselves within Bon Dieu's grace.

Lwa Rasin – translates as the root Lwa of your line, binding you to your ancestors both near and far. Your own ancestral root is what we are talking about here, where ever your family tree theoretically planted itself - i.e. in Europe, in South America. Rasin spirits are often spirits unique to a given locale. They are often (though not always) spirits who go back a long time in history. They can be spirits of the land where a family has lived for generations. They can be ancient family founders who are available for counsel and advice.

Over the centuries, your blood ancestors collected or engaged these spirits until they became specific to your bloodline. They belong to you, by right of your bloodline and you belong to them by the same claim. They are not ancestors, but spirits who walked with your ancestors. For example, if your family line is from Scotland, then you could have a spirit or energy that comes from that location as a *rasin* lwa. Or if you have Native American background, you could find a Southwest spirit coming forward to speak to you.

These spirits represent the area that your ancestors came from or settled in. They can be European, Asian, African, or any blend of your personal background. They are simply there. I think people who 'channel' spirit guides are actually tapping into this level of their personal spiritual escort.

Wonsinyon – means Escort spirits that accompany the Lwa Met Tet, and who modify the amplitude and frequencies of its vibration or presence. They are spirits who are both unique to the Met Tet's frequency as well as your own. They are not your ancestors. Those spirits are hard coded into your blood. Rather, these are spiritual energies that have chosen to walk with your Met Tet and by association, with you. It is up to you to discover both who they are as well as how they can assist you in your life.

Let's take a moment to review some of this and put it into a broader context. Vodou is a monotheistic religion. It recognizes a single Creator, the ultimate reality, vast, beyond our mortal comprehension. Totally feminine, totally masculine – all things, all states, All. There is often confusion about this point because some people think that the Lwa are worshipped. This is not so. We serve the Lwa, because they have a unique position in the hierarchy of the faith. They can bring our petitions right to the Source, thus enabling us to have our voices heard directly.

Below the Divine, are your Ancestors, your direct kinsmen. Each child is born into the lineage of his or her ancestry. Your personal lineage is encoded in your very blood. Vodou doesn't include as ancestors people who are not related to you. In some pagan paths today, Ancestors have become a catch-all phrase for anyone who inspired you in life. You may have been inspired by your Great Aunt, who is related to you by blood. She is a blood related Ancestor. Or you were inspired by Mickey Mantle. But unless Mickey is in your family tree, he is not an ancestor.

Each person comes into the world with an Escort, your personal spiritual posse as it were. The leader of this spiritual collective is the Met Tet, also called the Guardian Angel. This leader travels with a host of other spirits, all of whom have a vested interest in you, both in this life and beyond. This collection of spirits is the reason that one does not need to collect additional spirits. You do not select spirits because you feel called to them, you think their offerings are cool or you like pink, so Erzulie must be your Met Tet. You already have a multitude of spirits. Learning who they are, how to work with them and how to serve them is a lifetime of education.

These Escort spirits, those individual energy matrices which choose to walk with the Met Tet and you, are amplifiers of the Met Tet's energy. For instance, if you have Agwe, you might also have LaSiren or Erzulie Freda(his wives) or Ogoun Balendjo, Ogoun Badagris or Ogoun Ossange (His lieutenants). You can also have a variety of spirits from many nations. It is their choice, not yours, which is why we say it is in the blood and a life time of learning. But these are just the popular Lwa that one becomes familiar with in practice.

The concept of escorts is also a subtle knowledge of all the parts of ourselves that walk with us in life. To really understand this idea, think of escort spirits as a literal escort, a collection of spirits, walking before you or behind you, or next to you. Some are closer than others. They change positions over time, moving forward and backward.

Or, try this visual. Imagine yourself as part of a constellation in the sky. You are one of the stars or planets, in a unique pattern among the billions of other patterns out in the Cosmos. Your Met Tet is the boss of this constellation. They may or may not be the most prominent star. Perhaps, one of the other stars or planets is the larger presence – like having Jupiter as well as tiny Io. Io is the Met Tet, but Jupiter's influence is felt more, because Jupiter is bigger. Yet tiny Io directs the path of Jupiter. Each escort spirit reflects, enhances or amplifies the power, energy and influence of the Met Tet. The Met Tet is the boss of the escort. The Met Tet sets the tone for your personality, your challenges in life and what drives you. The Escorts determine how you express your personality, how you handle the challenges and where you get the energy that drives you. Knowing who your Met Tet is can help explain much of your own nature and situation in life.

Let me give you an example of the interaction of the Met Tet with the Escort. Agwe walks with several Ogouns, and at least one of his wives. These spirits accent his matrix, enlivening him and giving him energy when he needs it. There is a Houngan in our house whose Met Tet is Agwe. But he is also an Ogoun Ossange.

Though he may seem mild to some, he has a fierce temper when provoked. His bosses at work know that when something needs to be accomplished, they can call upon this man to do it – because he has the authority and the necessary energy to push people the right way, to achieve the end result. That "push" comes from his Ossange escort spirit. It is his Ogoun coming through, charging the horse with energy and resolve when necessary. Agwe steps back, to allow that escort full and front exposure when needed.

Escorts are a hidden source of power in Vodou. Over the course of your life, those spirits whose energies are not needed at one time or other will recede to allow others to move forward. This fluidity is at the heart of Escorts. I do not believe you ever lose what you have been given by God. But I do believe that at different times your life, different energies will come into play, called forth by the exigencies of your circumstances. I have met folks who seem to have very little energy around them. And I have met others who are quite "large" in their spiritual ardor. It feels to me at least, like they have a bigger collection of energies around them. By larger gang, I simply mean that like star constellations, some escorts are a tight pattern, while others spread out across the sky.

Escort energy can be felt in things like hunches, premonitions or dreams. Some people can easily express their escorts in a tangible manner. The big burly cashier who dissolves into tears at the slightest word probably has Freda in his escort. Or the engineer who tinkers with a problem until it is solved might have the endless energy of Ogoun in his escort.

Still others sense it in a variety of subtle, yet no less specific ways. This can manifest as the way you might warm up to a stranger in a coffee shop. That sense of familiarity could easily be a set of escorts between the two of you, who are connected in some fashion. Your Agwe recognize their Siren, or their Dantor senses your Ti-Jean. It is a kind of shared intimacy found among the Lwa themselves that reflects out into the world by allowing two strangers to share a laugh, a smile or an interest. We are the mirror of the spirits. In our lives, They seek Their own spiritual succor. In Their presence, we find our Divinity.

Much of the work of being a servitor is about finding out which parts of ourselves are in play and learning how to adapt to those parts. A further refinement of this would be that once you have learned all the various parts, you begin to draw on them for a particular outcome. This is all good and expected, but it can become abused.

Some people, once they learn how to call upon this team of spirits, go looking for others that may not be a part of themselves. It can become all about chasing down and expanding your influence through many spirits who work effectively. And there are many spirits who do work very effectively for a person they are not "attached to" in the true sense. We call these "pwen achte" and they are covered in the chapter on Lwa. But it also can become an obsession, resulting in the perpetual pursuit of power. Such a pursuit nearly always results in the loss of that power through the neglect of the escorts who came with you in the first place.

You cannot choose the spirits. They choose you. You may adore Erzulie, but She could have not the slightest interest in you. I think this is why many folks tire of the serving aspect. They are serving spirits who could care less. Erzulie will always take, but she will only give to those She is truly part of. The rest can serve Her forever, without getting any results of any kind.

It needs to be stated here that you do not gain a desired Spirit just by serving them or simply picking them out of thin air. I am always being told by a new person, "Oh I love Erzulie, I've made her an altar and she's been helping me!" Really? You think that spirit is the real Erzulie Freda, do you? The greater probability is that this spirit you think of as Freda is a 'mort' - a stray entity - who found a gullible source for offerings and is using you to get what it wants. Let me repeat -- the Lwa choose us, we do not choose Them.

No one has the authority to take control of any Spirit, unless that Spirit has been given to them by an authority the Spirits Themselves acknowledge (such as an Asogwe priest.) There are people the Spirits see as knowledgeable, grounded and powerful. To these very few folks, the Spirits will actually answer without prior arrangement. Other than those few, the Spirits pretty much do as they please.

This is why, from the Vodou view point, you should take good care of what is yours and yours alone, because your ancestors and those spirits who came here with you are your primary guardians and guides.

Learn about them. Read your personal histories, study the literature and the stories of the countries your forefathers came from. Learn about your Ancestors histories and you will begin to learn about yourself. I can sing with great passion, but playing a musical instrument has always eluded me. Yet, I have been fascinated by violins all my life. I didn't get it until my father shared that his Great-grandfather was a violin maker. Once I had learned this piece of my personal history, the passion for violins began to make sense to me.

Spend time before your ancestor altar and talk to them – out loud. You'd be surprised at the responses you will receive. Work with them. Instead of asking the Lwa for something, try asking your family first. They are here specifically for you. So rejoice in the collection that is walking with you. They will never steer you wrong. Let's look in detail at some of these folks, so you can get a handle on how to work with them.

We have discussed the soul of a person, so the next piece of the "Who am I?" puzzle is the Met Tet. We have talked a little about the Met Tet or "head master", but who exactly is this Spirit that is so involved with you? One of the primary teachings of our society is to learn your Met Tet's power and weaknesses, for you will also learn about yourself.

Your Met Tet is the energy that is closest to you in vibration and style. It is said that you are a reflection of your Met Tet, as they are of you. This brings home the Hermetic axiom of "As above, so below." We are a mirror of the heavens. There is even a song to Legba that says," O Creole, fathom the mirror." Creole meaning you, the person singing the song, look inward to find the real answer to your question. Explore the deepest parts of yourself, so that you may begin to know yourself and your reason for being in this world. This is the inscription on lintel of the Library of Alexandria in ancient Egypt: Know thyself, so that you may be one with the gods. This is not new information, but is a long held belief in occult circles. And it is as true for the Vodouisant as it is the hermeticist.

You are born into this life with a Primary Guardian Angel, a powerful spirit who watches out for you and helps keep your potentials on track. Your Met Tet is the primary note in the chord that makes you uniquely you. A better analogy was offered by Mambo Jolie Balendjo on her forum. She said "the Met Tet is the key in which the chord - made up of you and your escort - reverberates into reality as well as the unseen reality[16]."

The Met Tet's basic nature and personality is very often strongly revealed through the Met Tet's child. It is a give and take relationship. They are you and you are them. They bring along their stunning successes and their crashing failures. For instance, Ogoun requires that his children have a keen sense of how to use power, when it is appropriate and when it is not. Ogoun kids who abuse their positions are prone to pride and strife. They end up

[16] www.nileshaman,org, accessed 1/2004

having many, many challenges to overcome and are not always happy with the outcome.

Papa Danbala's children make excellent diplomats, and remarkable leaders. But they can be slow to act, just like the great serpent. Children of LaSiren or LaBalen appear to drift along in life, without hassles or conflicts. However, an aimless lifestyle can also lend a sense of unease and instability to their lives as well.

Your Met Tet is central to the total you. It is a positive exercise to learn whose child you are, and how to work with that particular energy. The stories of your Met Tet are in essence your stories. Your Met Tet's achievements are shining examples of encouragement for yourself. Likewise, your Met Tet's failures are warning beacons, to help you avoid the same pitfalls.

Each generation in your family had their own constellation of spirits that walked with them and helped them along the way. As each successive generation moves forward, a part of the previous generation's spirits become yours to work with. You inherit spirits – from your parents, from your grandparents. So now let's do the math. You have two parents, four grandparents, eight great grandparents, sixteen great-great grandparents. If you inherit just one spirit from each pair, all the way back through antiquity, you begin to get a sense of just how many spirits are walking with you in this life today. You may never know any of them, or you may get to know a few very intimately. Some may be better known at this time of your life and others will step forward later on as your life or needs dictate.

Papa Edgar told me that everyone's escort flexes and changes according to their lives. We aren't the same people we were in high school, or even college. So why wouldn't the spirits evolve with us? Maybe we need Ogoun Feray's fierce energy to study for final exams at 20 but (hopefully) we have grown and now at 50, we can call on Ogoun Ossange's calm, direct energy as we asses our place in the working world. It is the same matrix, just a different energy signal.

Think of the Lwa as diamonds, with many facets. Ogoun is the one we're talking about so let's examine, for a moment, the Ogoun diamond:

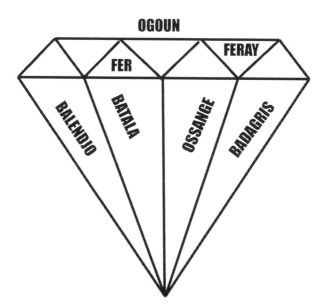

The entire diamond is Ogoun, but each facet represents a different matrix of the Lwa. There is the Feray facet, the fierce, angry warrior. There is the Obatala facet, the cool, calm lawyer. The Balendjo facet is the medical Ogoun, who is transmuted his warrior weapon into medical ones. The Badagris facet is the organizer, translating his ceaseless energy into organized files, list making and name taking. It is the same energy – the restless, ceaseless Ogoun -- but each facet cools and focuses one aspect of the Ogoun diamond.

Learning which facet or facets you carry allows you to hone in on that particular one and focus all its power, discipline and benefits in your life.

The idea here is that you don't go looking for spirits – you already have plenty of your own to work with. To adopt a spirit because you like them is to insult those who choose to be here with you. And that adopted one may not care about you at best or at worst, turn and do something you won't appreciate. These are not forgotten and remembered energies. They are sentient beings, alive and vibrant. Let's not insult them by treating them as party favors, to be picked up one day and discarded the next as we flit from path to path. Commit to learning about and from them, and they will return the gift tenfold. Ignore them at your peril, for they will turn their back and deal with you accordingly.

We discussed Escorts earlier – those spirits who choose to walk with you and your Met Tet. There is another class of escorts. The spirits themselves are also accompanied by Escorts -- their own. I mentioned before that if you have Agwe Tawayo, you also have LaSiren and Erzulie, because they are his wives. You also have his lieutenants, Balendjo, Badagris and Ossange. Each major Lwa is also accompanied by a cadre of lesser spirits who choose to walk with the Lwa. This same paradigm is in play in the heavens for the Lwa, as it is on earth for you. The companions you choose to walk with in your life, affect how you live that life. Your friends influence your choices on a range of things from the movies you consider seeing to the restaurants you all choose to visit. In other words, the physical constellation of your friends influences you and your life, just as the spiritual constellation that surrounds your Met Tet influences them.

And the idea of Escorts doesn't end there. The Rasin Lwa come with their own escorts, the Guédé with theirs – the lists are endless and mind boggling in their complexity. This interrelation of spirits is at the heart of the confusion regarding the Lwa. With so many connections, so many families and so many minor spirits along the way, most of the houngans and mambos I met in Haiti simply shrugged and said," So? It works. I do not need to know why or who. I simply know it all works, under God."

I like that attitude. Our Western minds want clean, compartmentalized organization. But Vodou resists and well it should. The living, breathing structure of the religion is anchored in its family roots, even among the spirits themselves.

Chapter Six: The Rada Lwa

We have spent a great deal of time speaking about the Spirits and how Vodou is all about the Spirits. So just who are these folks and how does one begin to get to know them?

People who come to me often state that they had a dream about someone they can only identify by their dress or their uniform. This person spoke a strange language the dreamer did not understand, but somehow seemed able to comprehend in some way. Often as not, the dream repeated, until finally, curiosity got the better of them and they began a search on the Internet for this person. And as often, that search led them to our web site and the page for a specific Lwa.

I have had folks as far away as Norway contact me about Lwa. A man in Oslo kept dreaming about a large boat, sailing up and down the fjord he lived near, with canons firing and a tall, dark man with green eyes giving orders. He found me on the web and contacted me, asking for help identifying this person. I related that I thought it might be Agwe Tawayo, the great Admiral of the oceans. So now, Agwe has himself a servitor in Norway, who keeps an altar on his deck, sings to him in Norwegian and is planning on kanzo in our house one day.

A man in Italy was dying of a brain tumor and dreamt of a soldier dressed in a red uniform, brandishing a sword. The uniformed warrior demanded that he serve him with whiskey and tobacco and told the dreamer that in exchange for a weekly service, he would save his life. The man did as requested and when he went for the next brain scan, the tumor was gone – as if it had never existed. The Italian served as best he could, but he found me and asked for help – he told me the name of his red warrior was Feray, and that he was devoted to him for saving his life. Awoche Nago Papa Ogoun! My Italian friend still lives his life, a happy servitor to his red spirit.

These and many other stories clearly tell me that the Lwa are omnipresent in the world. The Lwa cannot be contained by time or place, by land or by men. They choose who they wish to work with, and they work with whomever they choose.

Who are the Lwa of Vodou? Although they are often taken to be gods, they are not. In Vodou, there is only one God, the ultimate reality. So great and so vast is this presence, we cannot totally comprehend it within the limitations of our own mind. The Divine is all states of being – male, female, plant, animal, mineral. There is nothing greater than God.

Between the Manifest Divine and us are a host of other beings. In Vodou we call them angels, ancestors, entities, mysteries, spirits and Lwa. These beings serve the will and governance of the Divine and the movement of communication between us and the Divine. Some of these beings are non-human, some were once human and were elevated to the status of Spirit and some are not known to us on any level at all.

As I spoke of earlier, each of us has a specific set of these Beings who choose to walk with us in this life. We call them by a variety of names such as Lwa, Escorts, Met Tets and Rasin. But in the end they are all Spiritual beings of the non-manifest world.

The Lwa of Vodou are many things: energy patterns long established through prayer and ritual; entities that once were human; spirits that have never had corporeal bodies. Think of them as the ancestors of the human race, elevated to the status of Lwa or Saints. The Catholic Church continues to elevate simple human beings to supernatural status every year. Here in Philadelphia, we have the great Lwa Mother Katherine Drexel. She is a saint by definition of the Catholic Church, but a Lwa by any other name. People pray to her and serve her by going to mass, holding pieces of her clothing against their bodies and asking her to affect cures for them or family. The Catholic Church has taken note of the many miracles attributed to her, and canonized her. The Catholics revere her as a saint, but in the lexicon of Vodou, we would call her a Lwa. She is a human who has been elevated to supernatural status.

The Lwa are timeless, omnipresent and omniscient. They move through time and space to be where they are needed most and when they are needed. They rode on the shoulders and in the heads of their servitors during the Haitian Revolution. They make fun of the living during the days of Fet Guédé. And they lay down with their *hunyos* (spirit children) in the djevo during kanzo, assuring the candidates that they will be theirs forever.

There has been much written about the hot Petro spirits or the cool Rada Lwa. It is a mistake is to think of the Lwa as binary opposites - good or bad, hot or cool. These descriptions often reflect the "style" in which the spirit is served, more than the spirit itself. We humans attach these descriptors to the Lwa, creating the way in which they have become known.

Along with the styles of service, the groupings are an indication of the African origins of each nation. Rada spirits come from the West African coastline, and include the tribal affiliations of Arada, Dahomey, Senegal and Ibo. They are often descended from the royal houses of Africa, and so their services flow in the manner of a courtly arrangement.

The Kongo nation of spirits hail from the Kongo, but also include the Haitian born Lwa known as the Simbi nation. Their services are colorful, energetic affairs with danceable rhythms and many songs that have crossed into popular musical culture.

Petro is the name given to the spirits who had their genesis on the island of Haiti. It is thought that a slave named Dom Pedro gave his name to the style of service we now call Petro. The Lwa such as Erzulie Dantor, Ti-Jean Petro and Gran Bwa are all spirits who came into existence on the island of Haiti.

Think of these various nations as both the origin of the Lwa as well as their "styles of serving." For example, Ogoun is served both in the Rada nation and the Petro Nation. Bossou also has a Rada side and a Petro side to his services. There are many

Lwa that straddle both universes. This is not as strange as it might seem at first. There is a different ways of serving these spirits according to their individual natures and needs of the community.

Remember my diamond theory of the Lwa from the previous chapter? I used Ogoun as the example. The Ogoun diamond has many facets, each one a separate ray of the total gem we call Ogoun. Each ray (Ossange, Balendjo, etc.) has its own particular quirks, desires and abilities. Each facet requires its own style of service and offerings. Learning what all those facets require for service takes a lifetime of study and dedication.

Another way of thinking about styles of service is this: if the American Ambassador for the USA went to China, they would fet him Chinese style. But he would still be American; his basic country of origin would not change. Thus, Ogoun is always Ogoun, but in Rada service, we work one way and in Petro service, we work another. This is the reason why one doesn't just pick a Lwa and wing it - there is a right and a wrong way to do the work. Practicing Vodou is a lifetime of work, understanding and growth. The Lwa are here to help, but we must make the effort to approach service in Vodou correctly.

That said, we also have to acknowledge that the Lwa are in charge of the Vodou faith. They taught the Reglemen to the early Ancestors. They conferred the Asson, the emblem of priesthood, to the kanzo candidate. And they choose when and where they arrive in service. I can not count how many times we prepared someone to be the vessel of the spirit, only to find the Lwa choosing someone else entirely as their horse.

This willingness to be a part of their services is at the heart of the faith. A religion where the very spirits we pray to arrive and dance with us, is a direct and tangible event for those who are willing to move out of their comfort zones and be a part of something greater than themselves. Only in a few faiths of the East (such as Hinduism) is the Divine's presence made physically tangible to the believer.

I said earlier that the Lwa are sentient beings. Let me clarify. The Lwa are beings as I perceive of them. They may or may not be perceived as such by other people. To some servitors, they are great mysteries, unknown and unfathomable. To others, they are like little children, petulant and demanding. Still others think of them as great stories, with no real or tangible presence. But for me and for my students, they are real and present beings who make their likes and dislikes clearly known.

I also tend to think of them as great truths, expressed through the stories of their lives. These are not "remembered" gods or ancient deities, long forgotten and recently dusted off. These are spirits for whom service has been on-going. There is a large body of spiritual works that include prayers of invocation, songs of praise and morality tales featuring heroes and villains, beautiful maidens and powerful warriors. These individuals are all vying for attention, adoration and veneration, so they can receive the greatest reward possible – that of serving their Creator to the fullest capacity of Their own potential. These prayers, stories and songs are how we learn about them and about ourselves. Studying the stories, myths and legends of your Met Tet, how they reacted, what choices they made and what they did with their knowledge can give you a clear view to understanding yourself. If you can accomplish this, then you have learned one of the two great truths in the world.

The first truth is the one you carry inside yourself, what is known as Self Knowledge. Knowing who you are can make all the difference in how you walk in the world. Understanding this truth, allows you to understand the second great truth – that which is around you in the world. The saying goes Understanding the first (self-knowledge) can help you understand the second (the world). Another way of saying this comes from the Hermetic sciences: "As within, so without." The Lwa have engaged in this dialog for eons, and left behind a trail of knowledge for us to begin the journey to understanding. We merely need to engage with it, in order to fully comprehend its mysteries. And by engaging, I mean serving, praying and speaking with, to, and about the Lwa. Once you do, you will find they are not so different from us.

Some of the Lwa were once human (such as Ogoun Shango and Agassou). Some have never been incarnated on this earth (Marassa for example) while others are something we cannot define at all (Silibo Nouvavou). But one thing they all share is a desire to interact with us. During the course of possession, they do not startle their servitors with grand entrances. The Lwa most often arrive in possession with a smoothness that belies their power and ability. The dancing hounsi, who begins to stand taller and move with a different gait, morphs into the fierce Ogoun Feray, with furrowed brow and deliberate gestures. The tall masculine man at the back of the room starts a grooming ritual that becomes an elaborate toilet, as Erzulie Freda takes her place within his body. The subtle arts of dance, dress, make up and stance, all combine to bring the Lwa to the forefront of a service. They desire communion and like good friends, they do not wish to disturb the celebration, but choose to slip in and partake of the festivities alongside of us.

Their appearances are not relegated to fets and ceremonies either. The most frequent appearances of the Lwa are the personal ones, where they arrive for the benefit of you and you alone. This is not done by a possession, but by an appearance in the places where you are the most vulnerable. Such an occurrence can happen in your dreams, when your defenses are down and you are more 'open' to new things, new images and to the spirit world. The stranger walking by or calling out to you in your dreams is merely the Lwa reaching out to you, looking for communion with you. In our house I teach that we are the gates by which the subtle realms have egress into this world. Not by loud or startling methods, but through gentle and continuous effort.

Think about it. If you are startled by something, you probably would not be very open to experiencing it again. But a subtle and pleasant greeting, even by a stranger, tends to linger in the mind longer than a loud and obnoxious one. The gate by which the mysteries have entry into this world lies within ourselves. We need only be open to the possibility of someone knocking on that gate, and it will swing wide open.

The Lwa will also make their presence known in the world of men as well as in dreams. Becoming aware of the world around you, will give you a whole new view of just what you have been missing. The Lwa can be anywhere.

The policeman on the corner directing traffic? That is Ogoun, the military spirit. The secretary from the next office who loves pink? That is Erzulie Freda walking in the world. Got a child who cannot stay out of the water for any reason? You just might have LaSiren swimming through your living room. Once you understand the nature of the Lwa, their inner meanings and outer appearance, you will see that they are everywhere!

When I was approaching my first experience of Vodou, I was "stalked" by LaSiren. I saw her everywhere I went – as a car dealership logo, painted on the hood of a car in a parking lot, a huge three dimension sign on a ceramic studio. I live in Philadelphia, not exactly a hot bed of seaside communities or shops, so this was very interesting to me. LaSiren is a huge presence in my life, and continues to make appearances in the most unusual of places.

The Lwa have a specific order they appear in, during a Vodou ceremony. It is called Reglemen. It is the regiment by which the Lwa are invoked, and we follow it by reciting the Priye Ginen or Prayer of Africa at the beginning of a service. I find the Priye a good foot print to follow for all things in Vodou, so I will follow its order in the following discussions. Regelemen begins with the Rada nation of spirits.

The Rada nation represents Lwa who come straight from the West African area known today as Benin. Dr. Karen McCarthy Brown describes these Lwa as civilian or familiar in nature. Rada rites are said to be the cooler, more beneficent and magnanimous portion of the classic Vodou service.

Rada honors those Nations and Lwa who are familiar to the congregation, African in origin and royal in lineage. The Rada spirits tend to be more balanced, occurring in pairs. The primary or first Lwa is Legba, who is solitary in his being. He is followed by pairs such as the Marassa Dosu Dosa, the holy twins of the pantheon. They are followed by Loko and Ayizan, then by Danbala and Aida Wedo. The royal lineage is seen in Lwa such as Houngan Agassou who hails from central Africa and can be traced to the royal house of Abomey. The African origin can be seen in Agwe who has his counterpart in both Agé of West Africa; Sobo and Bade who were re-imagined in the New World from the African spirit named Hevioso.

Rada rites include the nations of Dahomey, Adja, Ibo and Seneka. The Lwa who are named during the Rada portion of the service roughly fall under these categories of nations. White is the preferred color of these nations, reflecting on their cool, royal heritage. Most Rada Lwa share the white color with a second one, to help identify them in services and art.

LEGBA, The Great Gatekeeper

The Primary Lwa in all Vodou services is Legba. He is the pivotal point of Vodou, representing the sun that enlightens the world. Gérard Férerè wrote," Legba is the most powerful and important of all the spirits. He is the mediator between Gran Mèt (Great Master – God) and the other Lwa. He opens the mystic way to those spirits who want to manifest themselves among human beings. He holds the key of the poto-mitan. All services start with the salutation due to him."[17]

We open all our services with a salute to Legba. Master of the crossroads, he is the word of God made manifest. Legba is probably the best known and most widely accepted of all the Lwa in the pantheon. He is involved in all the activities of human life. His name changes according to the rites or the task he fulfils. Legba is such an important Lwa that he has avatars for all the various Nations. It is said that there is a Legba Nago, Legba Ibo, Legba Petro and Legba Kongo. This is just one way of saying that there is a Legba for every nation of Lwa. Their names, their services and their secrets are all kept by their servitors.

Many of his praise names have been lost through antiquity, but still others remain, linked intrinsically to the tasks He performs. Milo Marcelin gives a thorough listing in his book, *Mythologie Vodou*. Some of the many Legbas listed are:

---

[17] Ferere, G.A. (1989). *Le Vouduisme Haitien*. Jamaica Plain: Saint Joseph University Press.

Legba A-Gbo-Nou-Kosou keeps the entrance of the houmfort. Legba A-Gba-Nou-Kou-Houe and Gangan Legba are charged to bring the ritual sacrifices to the Lwa. Houn Legba watches the entrance of the particular badji for each Lwa. To-Legba is appointed to serve a community and protect its members. Yeke or Yege Legba gives pwens, a special kind of magical power. Hounto Legba is the Legba of the drums. Legba Se is the Legba of prayers. Legba a Dou is the overseer of vèvès, Legba Eskalia Pemba is the Legba of the houmfort soil[18.] The list goes on and on. How many of these Legbas are still fetted each year would depend on the lineage of the house, their relationship with a particular spirit and the need to invoke each of these Legbas powers.

Legba is also the protector and guardian of the household. Our family members defer to Him for guidance, before taking steps to rectify problems. We ask that he open the way for the correct outcome and to close the door to any obstacles that would keep us from fulfilling our destiny.

Generally praised as Vye Legba (Old Legba), Legba Atibon and Papa Legba, he is the beloved opener of the way between this world, and the world of the Lwa. One of his many praise names is Gran Chemin, meaning Big Road. It is one of the mysteries of Vodou, that the road we walk toward Ginen is also the Lwa who opens the way. Legba is also referred to in song as the poto mitan,

---

[18] Gilles, J.(2009) *Roots, Rituals, Rememberance.*Davie, FL: Bookmanlit,

the very axis by which the Lwa enter the peristyle. He is simply the spine that supports the world of the Vodoun, and as such, is exemplified as the pole, the post, the center axis, the poto mitan of the world. His cane is one of his many symbols, hiding within its humble appearance his real place in the Divine order of the Lwa. He is the poto mitan of the pantheon, the bridge that the Lwa use to transverse into this realm.

Legba, as Papa Max Beauvoir puts it, is the Divinity that represents Humility and Communication. Humility is the a way of seeing a person's virtue or attitude. When you are humble, you are open to the opinion and views of others. When you are open, then you can communicate with others. These two things are elevated to the status of deity in Vodou through the auspices of Papa Legba.

Papa Max writes, "So humble and benevolent is Papa Legba that He never needs sacrifices of pigs, or bulls or a big feast to be done in His honor. He is happy with a modest cup of coffee, a fistful of grilled or roasted corn or peanuts, some tobacco that He smokes in a noticeably simple pipe made of little bamboo and corncob. He goes about constantly throughout the 'great road of Life', that is why He is also called 'Met Gran Chemin' or the Master of the great Road. He stops here and there at the entrances of every Houmfort, just the time to distribute graciously His thoughtful advises to Houngans and Mambos."[19]

---

19 communication with Papa Max, 1998

As the messenger Lwa, it is fitting to see that everyone has a Legba. My Legba is actually talking to you right now as you read this. Your Legba is interpreting what I am trying to say. So, in a sense my Legba is talking to your Legba. If I don't explain things completely, your Legba fills in the blanks. Legba facilitates understanding as He is the being of understanding, of comprehension and of sensitiveness. He is goodness made divine.

Papa Legba is usually envisioned as an old, old man, so old that he is bent over. Sometimes he is said to have a broken leg. He is also called "Legba Do Miwa", Legba on the Back of the Mirror, and mirror symbology is important with Legba. He loves the double entendre of mirrors – are we what we see in the mirror, or merely a reflection of who we are? A good meditation point!

Legba carries his baton and a straw bag called a djakout. Sometimes people say he is accompanied by a dog. For this reason he is identified with The Fool in the Tarot. That card features a young man accompanied by a dog and carrying a sack on his back. The image is the metaphorical vagabond heading off to see the world, with a humble dog for company. This is a fitting image for Papa Legba who is always envisioned as a wandering man.

Despite the seriousness of his duties and given his great age, Legba is typically of amiable disposition. He is much loved by the people who greet him as "Papa." Every day belongs to Legba. I generally refresh his altar and offerings on Monday, as well as my ancestors. If he is not your Lwa Met Tet, then you must ask Legba to open the way for your own Lwa Met Tet, so you can receive blessings from them. Legba loves Red, but as he is served in both Rada and Petro rites, his colors then become Red and White. His symbols include a pair of crossed keys, a walking stick or cane, and crutches. He is syncretized with Saint Anthony (the wandering saint, an allusion to Legba walking in the world), Saint Peter (for the keys he holds in hands to the Pearly Gates of heaven) and St. Lazarus (the old man on crutches, with dogs for companions). His feast days are January 1 (to open the New Year), June 13 (Feast of St. Anthony), June 21st (Feast of St Lazarus), June 29th (Feast of St. Peter) and any given Monday.

Legba will be happy with a cup of strong black coffee, and some tobacco for his pipe. However, like all Lwa, he does have a few preferences. He loves grilled/smoked chicken, grilled/smoked goat, sweet potatoes, white yams, bananas, any fresh fruit, black coffee (strong with no sugar). He likes pipes with tobacco, but I have also given him a really good cigar, and that seems to please him as well. I have a Legba djakout (a small, round woven bag, not to be confused with a regular djakout bag) I bought in Haiti hanging by the front door. It contains his pipe, his tobacco and a bottle of rum for him when he arrives.

Elsewhere, I have read that he likes mottled roosters, smoked fish, cassava, kleren, candy, guava, beans (white or red) and rice. In his Petro aspect he is given rum and foods liberally spiked with spices, Tabasco sauce or cayenne peppers.

If you are serving Legba (and just about everyone should), then there is a few details you need to know. First off, small, consistent actions are better than one large fet that cannot be repeated again. I urge you to make the smallest yet nicest offering you can for several reasons. One, you will be more inclined to do it regularly if it is a cup of coffee from the same pot you just made for yourself, than if you hike to the import store, to buy a very expensive brand, and then only do the offering when you have money again. And two, consistency is the key to getting the Lwa to actually aid you in your request. Use the same cup each time, place it in the same spot each time and after a while, the muscle memory of the action will make it effortless.

The Lwa love consistent behavior. I don't know why - they just do. If you change things each and every time, you can expect nothing to happen at best or something that you don't want to have happen at worst. Remember, Legba is the Gatekeeper. Like all toll takers, he has the right and the ability to close that door firmly in your face or open it wide and take off the lock, so it will never close again. I like having him on my side, so I urge you to be consistent and see what happens.

A very simple service to Legba would consist of getting a simple but clean china cup, a plain candle holder, a white candle, some coconut oil and a red cloth. Select a space that will not be disturbed by cats or kids or curiosity in any form. Clean the cloth, iron it and lay it out in this space. Place the china cup full of fresh brewed coffee on the cloth. Anoint the candle with coconut oil and place it in the holder. Sit before this space and clearly think of your intent in talking to Legba. Light the candle, and say

"Open the door for me Papa Legba, open the door.

Open the Door for me Papa Legba, Open the door.

Open the door for me Papa Legba, so I may pass.

When I return, I will salute you"

Sit quietly for a few minutes before this space and allow whatever images to arise. It may take a few tries, to quiet your mind, but images pertinent to your request will begin to arise in your mind. Make note of these. When you are done, you can allow the coffee to sit for a time, or take it to the crossroads, and toss it. Allow the candle to burn out. Pay attention to your surroundings after you have done this rite. You will find things pertinent to Legba – pennies on the sidewalk, older men with limps. The color red might begin to dominant your life. All these are good and warranted, for they are signs that Legba is manifesting around you. When you receive your request, then do the service again and thank Legba for his efforts. I always feel it is a good thing to be respectful and grateful. After all, he really doesn't have to do anything for us at all. It is His prerogative as a trickster spirit to open doors or to close them. I am grateful that he seems to always do as I request, but then, I do serve him Haitian coffee!

The Marassa: The Sacred Twins

After Legba in service, come the Marassa. There are many Marassa in Vodou and they are always accompanied by the: Dosu or Dosa, which are not twins, but are the children born after the twin birth. The term "dosou (dosa)" is derived from the Fongbe docu, meaning the child of either sex born after twins. In African-based cultures, the twin birth is not considered "finished" until the Dosu (a male) or Dosa (a female) is born. In the case of triplets, the last child is the Dosu or Dosa[20]. This is all part of the oblique knowledge about one and one equaling three in Vodou theology. Two things come together and create third or higher note of the original two. For example, a musician and his instrument create music. An artist and her medium create art. The two people come together and create a third life between them. That is what I mean when I say one plus one equals three. In Vodou, this formula is called Marassa.

Other notables are Marassa Twa (Triplets), Marassa Bwa, Marassa Kreyol, Marassa Ile (Nago Twins), Marassa Petro and Marassa Bwa Makak. The Shouket is the child born before twins and Idogwe is the second child born after twins. Children born with extra digits are called Avelekete (multi-fingered child). Those born with a head full of curly hair are Marassa Dada. These are all considered to be a powerful child, and are magically aligned with the Marassa[21.]

The Marassa are divine children, but they are more ancient than any other Lwa. In a private conversation with Met Agwe, I was told that the Marassa came first after Legba, but were so God-

---

[20] Houlberg, M. (2011). Two equals three. In P Peek (Ed.), *Twins in Affrican and Diaspora Cultures: Double Trouble, Twice Blessed* (pp. 271-289). Bloomington: Indiana University Press.
[21] Ibid

like in their physical bodies that they are more like God than man. They sit between the worlds, in a place that few can venture. They are filled with Divine love, but are not of this plane, and so they act childish, having neither the form nor the ability to change out of their primeval attitude. Both Light and Dark, they exist before all and not at all.

Milo Riguad says they are "Love, truth and justice. Mysteries of a liaison between earth and heaven, they personify astronomic-astrological learning. They synthesize the Vodou Lwa as personification of divine power and the human impotence. Double the life of any Lwa or human, they have considerable power which allow them to manage people through the stomach. They are child-like mysteries." [*hence their insatiable appetites - Mambo*].[22]

The Marassa are somewhat different than other Lwa, in that they are not channeled through possession in Vodou ritual. They are too old, too large, too omnipotent to be able to come down into this earthly vessel we call the body. Their presence would burn up the vessel, leaving behind nothing but a shell. Yet, their importance in the Vodou pantheon becomes clearer when you think of the Vodou Trinity. The core trinity of Vodou service is the Lwa, the Ancestors, and the Marassa.

---

[22] Riguad, M. *Voodoo Diagrams (1974) Voodoo Diagrams & Rituals*. New York: French & European Publications.

Seen as duality in action, they represent the totality of creative powers that are both expansive as in creating the universe, as well as contractile such as death or dying. They are powerful in the areas of general luck, fertility, and are particularly able to bring rain. They are also well-known for giving the gift of clairvoyance, which is referred to simply as "eyes." Many songs in the Vodou corpus refer to this:

Gen je O, Marassa, Lwa-yo, Gen je O!

Gen je-O, Marassa pou nou gade yo vle!

The Marassa have eyes, All the Lwa, have eyes!

The Marassa have eyes, for all of us to see!

The Marassa represent abundance, blessings, the gift of children, the sacredness of family and the mysteries of the Divine. The Marassa also represent special births, such as three children, or children born with a caul on their face. The sacred Twins are invoked at the beginning of every service along with Papa Legba, for without the Marassa, nothing can come into existence. Their combined magic produces the abundance of the world (that one and one equals three formula again).

The Marasa are most commonly syncretized with the Saints Cosmos and Damian in the Rada rites, and the Virtues or "Three Egyptians" when served in Petro. Like all sacred Twins, they are identical, yet sexless. They are Potential, therefore, they contain every potentiality on earth: male and female; light and dark; positive and negative; all opposites, all identical.

They love to eat and will resort to trickery to get an even larger meal served to them. Many songs sing about them hiding during a ceremony and then coming out to complain they received nothing to eat:

Kou sevis komanse, li pase deye kay

Kou sevis la fini, li di li pa manje!

The service began, they went behind the house,

The service finished, they said they did not eat!

The song also signifies their powers. The twins are associated with transitional places such as thresholds and their magical powers are so strong they can protect the most mystical and magical of places, the crossroads, where the world above, meets the world below. By placing them at the beginning of the service, we have the full spectrum of ages – Old Legba and the young Marassa, both of whom have the power to open the spiritual road of the service.

The belief and power of Twins comes directly from Africa, where the cult of twin births is very strong. According to Marilyn Houlberg, the Creole word for twins, "Marassa" is derived from the KiKongo word *mabassa* which means those who come divided, or the one who comes as two. The Fon cosmology in particular is so penetrated by dualism, that Fon concepts of twins and other sacred children merit special attention .Some African groups have a fraternal twinning rate four times that of their European neighbors. Even their creator Divinity Mawu-Lisa is a twin. As Paul Mercer noted in 1954:

"The ideal type of every group in the divine world is a pair of twins of opposite sex or more rarely, of the same sex. We have pointed out that among men also the ideal birth is a twin birth and that in the beginning every birth was of that kind. This twin structure of the gods is the rule."

The Marassa sit at the top of the Priye Ginen and herald the many twinned pairs of Rada Lwa that follow them in the listing. It is one of the hidden codes about the Rada Lwa. The oldest and most revered of the Rada mysteries come as twins, and give their energy as a balanced set of blessings.

Various Catholic saints are used to image the sacred twins. The most popular are the twin saints Cosmos and Damien. In Haiti, the palm fronds they hold in their hands are interpreted as curative leaves for medicines. The other pair is St. Claire and St. Nicholas. These two saints parallel the West African sky deities Mawu-Lisa. Mawu is seen as female and associated with the moon; Lisa is seen as male and associated with the sun.

In Vodou, Saint Claire is associated with the moon, because of the moon-shaped host she holds in a monstrance, the chalice-like device used in Catholic churches to display the sacred host of communion. Saint Nicholas is connected with the sun, for the sun like imagery on his vestments in the chromolithograph (color paper images of the saint ubiquitous throughout all of Haiti) of him. At ceremonies for him, particularly on his feast day of December 6th, Vodouisants pray to him while facing east toward the rising sun. This link between saint, sun and twins is expressed in the invocation for Saint Nicholas that accompanies the vèvè for the Marassa. Roughly translated:

> *"By the power of Saint Nicholas, the sun of justice, who shines on the four corners of the earth. By the power of Marassa Dosu Dosa, Marassa Zin Sou, Zin Sa, Marassa (guardian of the) bush, Marassa (guardian of the) house, Marassa of Africa Ginen. Ago, Agosi, Agola."*

Those servitors who honor the twins often find their work "doubled", a subtle reminder of the power of the Twins to bring things into fruition twice. They are very jealous, so when serving them be sure to offer identical things: sweet sodas, candies, popcorn and dolls. Place their offerings on identical plates or on banana leaves, on the floor, so like the children they are, they can eat with their hands and enjoy their offerings at their leisure. If offering toys then be sure there are two identical ones, or you will wish you had. They are not children per se, but they are childlike in their attitude. Think of kids on Christmas morning who don't get an equal share of gifts!

This child-like demeanor should be your guide to serving them. In Vodou we use the plat Marassa which is a 1, 2, or 3 portioned plate for their food offerings. In Haiti, we also had the twinned vessel for liquids as well. Find double glasses, double portion plates (you can find them in kiddie colors in Kids-R-Us or other stores catering to the needs of children) and divided plates for their food offerings. Marassa Ibo take their offerings on china plates. Marassa Nago eat off tin plates. Marassa Dosu Dosa eat off earth ware plates. And the Marassa's offerings are always placed on the floor, often on top of banana leaves.

You can offer them coffee, but make sure one has sugar and the other one does not. They eat chicken or pigeon. Candies, fried sweet bananas, rice with red beans, rice cooked with coconut milk and dusted with cinnamon are also some of their favorites. Serve them kola champagne(a super sweet cola soda), fruity drinks, water and syrup such as grenadine or almond.

The Marassa are associated with the number three (in spite of being twins) and their color(s) are pale blue and pink. Their day of the week is Wednesday and their feast days are January 2nd and September 26th.

If you have twins in your family, it is considered important to serve the Marassa. They are seen as having blessed you with their physical presence. Keep twin dolls on your altar as a focal point for working with the Marassa. And serve them if only if you keep to the schedule or They will be offended and perhaps, make your life a challenge you do not wish to have!

Papa Loko: Lwa of Healing

The mystery we call Papa Loko is one of the most important Lwa in the Vodou pantheon. Loko is the father of the initiates, the mystical healer of the temple and a just judge. Loko plays a central role in the cycle of the initiation of Houngans and Mambos. He is one of the oldest and most powerful mysteries, holding knowledge not only of the kanzo, but of leaves and herbs, medicines and cures as well as judgments and decisions. After Legba and Marassa, in our house, we call Papa Loko. He is the primal or first houngan, and is likened to an invisible presence that has authority in every peristyle throughout the world. It is via Loko that sacred knowledge is conferred to the hunyos during a kanzo. Many Vodou songs speak of Papa Loko as the "Houngan of all houngans":

> *Bonswa Papa Loko houngan mwe.*
>
> *Bade wandile gwetò Lisa dole-zo!*
>
> *Apre Bondje mwen lan men o;*
>
> *Rele Dje, a mwen lan men ou la.*
>
> *Bondje devan ou pa we, Le sen deye-o!*

> *Good evening Papa Loko my houngan.*
>
> *Bade wandile gwetò, Lisa dole - zo*
>
> *After God, I am in your hands,*

Call God, I am in your hands.

God before can't you see, the Saints' after.[23]

This song reminds the congregation that, despite how powerful the Lwa may be, it is always God who comes first. Most of Papa Loko's songs contain *langaj*. In the above song, the line "Bade wandile gwetò Lisa dole-zo" is considered to be *langaj*.

Papa Loko is known to be the Lwa of leaves, particularly leaves that confer healing. It is said that he knows all the properties of the leaves and herbs of the forest for both medicine and magic. Haiti has a term for someone who is skilled in herbal medicine. That term is "leaf doctor," a reference to the individual's knowledge of medicine leaves and their application. Leaf doctors are the resident healers in rural Haiti. Where western medical skills are rare, particularly in the mountains, a good leaf doctor can truly save lives and help the sick to heal. Due to his extensive knowledge of the pharmaceutical uses of herbs, Papa Loko is the best qualified medsin fey or leaf doctor to call upon when ill.

Loko is also called the spirit of the wind and is said to fly like a butterfly on the breezes. This ability to float in and out of temples like the insect gives rise to the theory that he listens in on people without their knowledge. He hears all the good and the bad in the world. This gives Loko the ability to make judgments and it is said he can settle any dispute fairly for both parties. Loko is a

[23] Fleurant, G. (1996). *Dancing Spirits*. Westport, CT: Greenwood Press.

carrier of messages, and a channel of communication among his devotees. Here is an older song that speaks of Loko as a butterfly who brings messages:

Papa Loko mwen se van, Vo ale mwen se papion

Map pote nouvel la pou yo

Sa ki di bein an ge-m la m'ap gade o

Sa ki di mal la ge-m la m'ap gade o

Vo ale mwen se papion, Ma pe pote nouvel la pou yo

Papa Loko, I am the wind, I am the butterfly,

send your message through me,

I shall bring it for them.

Those who speak sweetly about me, I see them.

Those who speak badly about me, I see them,

I am the butterfly, I will bring it for them.[24]

Because the wind blows everywhere, Loko is acknowledged as both a messenger and a herald who announces things to the congregation. As a cosmic spirit, Loko has the power over the wind as well as the rain. When he is not happy, he brings bad weather and tornadoes.

---

[24] LaGuerre, M. (1980) *Voodoo Heritage.* New York, NY: Sage Publications. p. 90

Loko is known to be very strict regarding lineage tradition. When things are not being executed properly, be it salutes, *vres* (ritual salutation performed in service) or even just the positioning of the hounsi in service, Loko will arrive in possession and be very stern with his corrections. He can be harsh when things are not being done properly. However, Papa Loko is as a fair arbitrator whose decisions are likely to settle disagreements among the congregation. They call upon him to make a judgment, knowing he will be fair and right. More often, a single servitor will call upon Loko to settle matters as mundane as field usage and as complicated as love. The servitor knows they have the right to call upon Loko for this work. This is an extension of his function as messenger. The messenger is the one capable of determining whether the message is true or false, by his good judgment:

Papa Loko jige reson an

Apre delis Papa Loko nap tande nouvel

Papa Loko, judge us,

After your judgment, we will know who was right.[25]

Loko's origins are not clear. In Haiti, Loko has a diverse range of possible roots that suggest both his names and his associations. Loko is known for giving traditional knowledge. According to Vodou tradition, it is Papa Loko who confers the asson

---

[25] *LaGuerre, P. 91*

to the initiates, elevating them to the status of Mambo or Houngan. This handing over of the asson has a mythical origin in the beginning of Haiti's history where it is said that in a cave "it was an Indian who offered it to an African, while sharing the lands' secrets with him."[26] It has been also said that the name 'Loko' comes from the ancient Taino who called themselves *Loko-no* or sons of Loko, the mythical founder of the Arawak bloodline in the Orinoco from "whence these set out to conquer the Caribbean islands."[27]

Loko's possible African origins are no less intertwined with myth and legend. Some writings state that his name is derived from the Iroko tree of West Africa. Given that Loko is associated with trees, this linkage makes for an interesting connection. Some scholarship points to his legends coming out of Dahomey where he is one of the royal ancestors of the clan Adja. Here his two principle avatars are found: Loko Attisou from Hula, and Atidan or Adan Loko from Oweme. And there has been a nation of people called Loko in Sierra Leone for over two centuries. So from where ever Loko came, his mystery is strong, beloved and holy in Haiti.

Loko is saluted following the Marassa in Reglemen. The presiding priests wear golden kerchiefs about their shoulders when saluting Loko and all priests, both mambos and houngans

[26] *Conversation with Houngan Andre Basquiat. (2008).* Bel Air, Port-au-Prince, Haiti
[27] Beauvoir_Dominique, R. (2007) The vodou-makaya artistic tradition in haiti's heritage. In Mathez, P. & Hainard, J. (Ed.), *Vodou: A Way of Life* (pp 167-174) Geneve: Infolio/Musee d'ethnographie de Geneve.

stand out of respect for this great Lwa. Once Loko has been saluted, then all mambos and houngans present are also saluted, to demonstrate their rank in the hierarchy.

Loko owns the asson and therefore the language of the asson. This special language is called *"tolke"* and it is a series of mirrored gestures that display both the asson's voice as well as the prowess of the priest in talking through the asson. It can be a light hearted conversation or it can be a challenge, with ever more complicated gestures demanding equally obscure answers. However it is done, it is the method by which priests recognize one another. When a priest calls another one forward, they have no choice but to stand and respond in kind.

The Vodou religion recognizes at least five manifestations of Papa Loko, of which four carry the tools associated with the Vodou priesthood. Loko Attisou carries (and therefore gives) the asson, the sacred emblem of the priesthood. Loko Azanblo carries a straw sack full of medicinal leaves and a kwa-kwa rattle (maraca). This Loko arrives to consult with people about their various problems. Loko Attidan carries the sacred collar (kolye) of the initiate and oversees the proper tying of the collar. Loko Mayifado carries the iron bell called ogan or agogo. This bell was originally a large hand bell with internal clapper used to call certain Lwa. In the north of Haiti, the giving of this bell involves an initiation called "priz de klosh". Finally, Azagon Loko is called the "father" or oldest manifestation of the other four. He is the root of Lokou, the lineage from which Loko descends.

Loko's color(s) are white, gold/golden yellow/mustard yellow, and light green. His sacred day of the week is Wednesday and his feast days are January 6th (the Epiphany in the Catholic calendar of observances) and March 19th (Saint Joseph's feast day). He is also commonly feted on the anniversary of the founding of an houmfort.

Loko's Catholic saint association is Saint Joseph, the father of the Christ child, which mirrors Loko being the father of the initiates. Loko is commonly represented by the image of a red rooster.   His tree repository is the holy mapou tree (ceiba pendantra, ceiba bombax), or the cypress.

Loko drinks kleren, rum, beer, or trempe and coffee with sugar. He is offered palm oil, popcorn, rice with various beans (red kidney beans, pigeon peas, and lima beans), rice with mushrooms, corn meal boiled with black beans, yams, and pumpkin soup to name a few foods. He receives blond or red roosters and red bulls. His food may variously be boiled, fried, or broiled.

Like Legba, Papa Loko's offerings are often placed into a bag called *latanier* which is made from the fan palm and hung in the mapou tree, which is his repository, though he may also be served in gourd dishes. Like all Dahomean royalty, no one is allowed to see Papa Loko eat. Papa Loko enjoys his pipe and tobacco, and a walking stick (baton Loko), which he never actually leans upon. Beloved of the temple and the sosyete, his possessions are few but when he does comes, it is with purpose and function.

Ayizan: The Mother of the Initiates

Where we regard Loko Atissou as the father of all kanzo initiates, Ayizan is the Mother of all Initiates. Ayizan Velekete is her full name, and she is often seen as a very old woman, with an apron that has deep pockets.

Ayizan's origin is through an old Dahomean Divinity. Her name comes from the Fon people of Benin, where Ayi means earth or land. Zan means sacred. The name is doubled, as *Vele* is a word from the Mina people and it too means sacred, as does *kete* which means land. So her name is a double of Sacred Land.

Mambo Ayizan Velekete governs the marketplaces of the world. Her control of the marketplace is symbolic of her power to manage transactions between the physical world and the world of the spirits. I think sometimes this action is why some temples pair her with Legba, the gatekeeper and not Loko, the healer. Although she does govern both functions, Ayizan is more often seen as the mother who rules the djevo, the birthplace of initiates. This rulership over the djevo makes Ayizan the first mambo.

Her symbol is the Royal Palm tree, used extensively during her ceremonies. An unopened palm frond is cut for both the ceremony of *Chire Ayizan* (shredding of the royal palm leaves) and *Kouri Ayzian* (the running of the royal palm) key parts of the initiatory cycle, enfolding the new initiates in the protection and purity that she conveys. Ayizan brings the mysteries of the Kanzo and of life and death to us here in the Marketplace. The Yoruba tradition refers to the earthy plane as the Marketplace, so it is fitting that Ayizan is the one who brings them down to us.

The palm is a fitting symbol, standing tall and erect. It symbolizes both righteousness and integrity. The unopened palm frond symbolizes purity and cleanliness. And the hard trunk of the tree projects the idea of force. This combination of ideals – righteousness, fortitude and force, all come together in the djevo when the candidates are brought forth as new kanzos, exemplifying these virtues of the faith.

Her vèvè is comprised of her initials, the "A" and the "V", intersecting across each other. The vèvè is sometimes further decorated with stars and whirls to imitate the royal palm frond, shredded and worn by every initiate of Vodou.

She is one of the oldest Lwa, whose roots lie in old Dahomey where she was a tutelary Lwa of the separatist clan Aladahouno. There her symbol is a mound of earth, fringed with palm fronds. In Haiti, she is served with palm fringes laid on a chair draped with a clean, white cloth. This "throne" may very well be a trace memory of her ancient, royal roots.

Chromolithographs of Christ, usually Christ being baptized by Saint John are used in association with Ayizan. Some temples use the image of Saint Claire, holding a glowing monstrance. Her physical symbol is the royal palm branch, frayed and covering her face. This branch is carried into the djevo and a section is also attached to the poto mitan. There, it symbolizes Ayizan's presence to anyone who comes under the tonnel and sees it attached to the poto. New born kanzo initiates all wear her palm fringe across their faces as they exit the djevo. This is to shield them during their first movements in the temple, and as a sign that they are eternally under her protection.

Ayizan's number is seven; her color(s) are white and silver. Her sacred day of the week is Wednesday and her feast day is January 6th. Ayizan's tree repository is the Royal Palm (roysontea regia) and it is the young shoots that provide the palm fringe (also called an Ayizan) that symbolizes her. Her Catholic saint associations are Saint Claire, Saint Rose, and occasionally Saint Martha (with dragon).

Ayizan drinks beer or *trempe*, raw cane liquor laced with aromatic and medicinal herbs. Ayizan is served properly with a royal palm fringe. She smokes a pipe with tobacco and may occasionally carry a straw djakout. Her offerings are placed in calabash gourd dishes (known as "kwi"), in a djakout or on banana leaves. Most of her services and ceremonies are secret, so there is not much that can be shared about this magnificent Lwa.

Danbala Wedo: The Creator Serpent

Danbala is the oldest of the Rada pantheon, and retains most if not all of his African attributes. In Dahomey, the Fon people have a great serpent god who is seen as a rainbow named Danh, the son of Mawu-Lisa. This serpent encircles the whole world with his tail in his mouth, representing unity and wholeness. This god, also called Da orders the whole cosmos. Da has a dual nature rather than a female-male identity. When he appears in the rainbow, the male is the red part of the rainbow, the female the blue. The stories of Da say that above the earth Da has 3500 coils, called asa-xasa, and the same number of coils beneath the earth; together the coils support the world. Da is the name given to this god in action, Mawu-Lisa is the name given to the god in thought[28]. This duality of spirit is what came into Haiti with the slaves.

The Empire of Dahomey was at its height around 1750. The Lwa we now call Danbala, or Dan-Ayida Wedo has two sources. The first source is Aida Hwedo from Abomey. This spirit is represented as a sky deity, travelling with thunder bolts as seen on the brass plaques of the royal palace at Abomey today[29]. The second is Dangbe` from the town of Whydah[30]. This spirit was also seen as both male and female, although in speaking of him, male gendered pronouns were used. Both shared the same attributes we recognize as Danbala today: whiteness, wisdom, fecundity, abundance, fertility and rain. These two spirits held similar positions but with one very important distinction. Dangbe` was the repository of the "common" ancestors, those spirits who were the descendants of non-royal families. Aida Wedo was seen as the

---

[28]*http://www.uned.es/geo-1-historia-antigua-universal/egipto_magia_amuletos%205_Wadjet_cobra.htm,accessed 9/12/2007*
[29] Spring, C. (1993) *African Arms and Armor.* Washington DC: Smithsonian Institute Press.
[30] Wills, J. (2001) *1688: A Global History.* New York: W.W. Norton & Co.

repository of "royal" ancestors[31]. The African tradition dictated
that these two classes never mixed. My guess is that during the
middle passage, the majority of slaves taken were "common" not
"royal." It stands to reason that 'royal' female prisoners of war
would either be placed in the king's harem and 'royal' males would
be killed. Priests were kept, in order to capture the gods being
served. This left the common folks - militia, farmers and others for
trade and export to the New World. Therefore, I forward the thesis
that Dangbe is a possible source for the Lwa we now call Danbala,
and Aida (Ayida) came to reference His female aspect.

I think of Danbala as the original astronomer or astrologer.
There are numerous stories of his passage across the night sky,
leaving a trail of scales that shine like stars. He has perfect
knowledge of the heavens, having learned this from the African
tradition called Na-Go Oyyo. In synthesis, he personifies fire and
water. Fire represents his serpent powers of regeneration and
creation. Water represents his deep knowledge or *konnesans* of the
world and its people. A fitting analogy, as he is served both in Rada
and in Petro. I have heard older houngans refer to him as the
Feather Serpent. These are not feathers like a bird has, but the
feathery trail of flames he carries as he moves into the world.

I keep white satin pakets for Danbala on my Rada altar. As
a Lwa who carries the ancestors, Danbala is served with pure
white, the color of ancestors in Africa. His pakets are decorated in

---

31 Hutton, C. (1821) *The Tour of Africa*, London: Baldwin, Cradock and Joy.

satin, with a crucifix sticking out of the top. I keep Danbala's paket with Freda's, as he is one of Freda's three husbands. In the ever dizzying set of relationships that make up the theology of Vodou, Danbala is often paired with Aida, but is married to Freda. Danbala Wedo's colors are white, with Aida often given white and black. In Haiti, it is traditional to offer her a black and white cow.

Danbala's day is Thursday while Monday and Tuesday are Aida's days. They take white foods as offerings. White chickens, white eggs, white rice, a saucer of milk, an egg on a mound of white flour, anisette liquor, white cakes and pastries, white wine, rice pudding, meringue cookies, bananas, white grapes, champagne, corn meal dumplings, coconut meal. In Haiti, I have seen houngans drop raw eggs and corn syrup at the poto mitan for Danbala. He never fails to arrive in possession of his servitor or 'chwal' (horse in Creole) and lick it all up.

Danbala's Catholic image is Saint Patrick for the snakes at the feet of the saint or Saint Moses for the story of Moses staff turning into a serpent in front of Pharaoh. Our Lady of the Immaculate Conception is used for Aida because of all the multi-colored cherubs in the picture. I personally serve Danbala with white anisette, corn syrup, white silk roses and white snake skins. I keep His badji filled with white crosses, white rosaries and those spotless white pakets that I make for his pleasure.

Agwe: Sovereign Sailor of the Seas

After Danbala, we call upon Agwe, the great Admiral to come and bless our services. Agwe holds a special place in our house, as we have many marine Lwa, beginning with the Houngan! Agwe loves the open sea, its colorful ports of call and the many lovely women he keeps in those ports. His servitors rassemblé (assemble to serve) him in many ways. Most Agwe children work or live near the ocean. They are sailors, boatmen and fishermen, people who make their living on or by the water. Surfers, divers and oil riggers are some of the many ocean occupations you will find Agwe working at. In Vodou He most often manifests as a great admiral. Taking a chair and rowing it around the poto mitan, he barks out orders and commands a great presence. He loves the ladies, and Agwe can always be seen with a couple of ladies perched on his lap, as he calls for rum and his spyglass.

It is said that all the sunken treasure ships, all the gold and material goods that have found their way into the deep waters of the world, belong to Agwe. Agwe is also the patron of fishermen, sailors and everyone who makes a living on the water. As the patron of all sea-going folks, he is specifically called upon under the name "Koki lanmè" (shell of the sea).

Agwe Ta'Woyo is the also the majestic magician of the seas and all its metaphysical meanings. Emotions, intuition, psychic abilities and depth of feelings are all part of his domain. His jurisdiction rules not only all things represented by the sea, but also that which sails upon the oceans as well. By virtue of his association with the Lwa Sobo and Bade, he commands the winds that blow over the oceans of the world including hurricanes, wind tunnels and all other manifestations of wind and water. In doing so, he controls the actions of the waves and their ceaseless energy. Agwe rules over tides, which also gives him a connection with the moon, too. All this demonstrates the huge arena of influence this mighty man of the sea has under his jurisdiction.

Agwe is also associated with the dark depths of the ocean. In occult terms, Agwe is the deep psychological intuition we all carry within ourselves – intuitive knowledge is his realm in the mind. No wonder we all love to sit and think by the water – that is Agwe reaching out to us on the salty breezes and rolling waves, hypnotizing us with his endless energy and power.

In Haiti, an island country with a large fishing industry, Agwe is often envisioned as light-skinned mulatto man with green eyes. Houmforts who serve him keep an admiral's coat and hat ready to dress Agwe when he arrives in possession. Agwe is married to LaSiren, the beautiful mermaid. His marriage to the Lwa of intuition pairs his own innate talents to Siren's psychic ones. But he also keeps the equally lovely Erzulie Freda Dahomey as a concubine, providing her with many gifts of gold and pearls, the products of his many trips over the seas. His affair with Freda is the manifestation of his own sexual potency as keeper of the fertile depths of desire.

Agwe has a large retinue of escort spirits in his wake, fitting for a grand master. They include Jeneral Klemyel, Klemezin

Klemey, Ogoun Balindjo, Agasou and Silibo, primarily. But Gran-n Erzulie and Erzulie Freda also walk with Agwe bringing their escorts as well. Some of those include Severin bel Fanm, Filomiz, Mambo Sesil (Saint Cecile), Mambo Dayila, Mambo Nana. These escort have a common origin, being water or sea spirits.

Agwe is associated with Agbe, the water spirit of Alada in Old Dahomey. There is scholarship pointing to his origin being from the West African town of Whydah, in relation to the spirits called Hu and Adantohoe, both of whom have similar characteristics and domains.[32]

I also enjoy the stories of Agwe that pair him with the Nephilim, those mythical beings who are said to be the progeny of angels and humans. This is shown by both legend of his birth (a fish and a human), his escort (Agassou and Silibo are both thought to be Nephilim) and his straddling of two universes – water (intuition) and material wealth (base or animal nature). However he came into existence, his staying power is strong and his ability to confer gifts of knowledge, wealth and abundance remarkable.

A conch shell horn is blown to signal Agwe during a Vodou service. Upon his arrival, he should be greeted with misting sprays and fanning, to keep him cool and comfortable. Failure to do so will result in his becoming overheated. At that point, Agwe will either become angry or simply withdraw from the ceremony.

---

[32] Herskovitts, M. (1958). *Dahomean Narrative.* Evanston, IL: Northwestern University Press.

In possession, Agwe does not speak, nor does he stand or dance. Rather, he is seen in his boat (a small chair with a cane for an oar), rowing around the peristyle to visit those present. His formal services begin in the peristyle and end with the society moving to the beach to complete the service. or even sailing out over the ocean. Once in open water, a *bak d'Agwe* (a small boat or tray) is filled with all sorts of food and liquor offerings, placed on the water at the height of the service. When it sinks, it is believed that Agwe has accepted the offering and will bless the sosyete for the gift.

Agwe Tawayo's color(s) are white, navy blue, or (in some lineages) green. His sacred day of the week is Thursday and he can be feasted annually any time between June 1st and mid-August, and again between December 12th-14th. His Catholic saint association is Saint Ulrich, for the fish held in the hand. But he is also one of the Lwa that is currently undergoing a renaissance in art and mysticism. At one time, a wooden model ship suspended from the roof of a peristyle was a symbol that Agwe was present in a given temple. Today, you will find images and statues of Neptune, Poseidon and even images of Michael Phelps used as symbols of this great man of the sea.

Agwe's feast is like a high tea party. In Karen Richman's wonderful *Vodou and Migration*, she details a high service done for Agwe in Leogane, Haiti. The feast was held on the beach, under a tent made from lace cloths. A long table was set with white linens, fine china and dainty pastries, cakes and candies. Champagne, white wine and coffee were served along with petit fours and finger sandwiches. The feast was seen as a success not just for the number of people who turned out but for the type and quantity of food offered. No small feat in a place like Haiti.

Because of his special status as a big Lwa of the Rada pantheon, his services should be very formal and lush affairs. Large tables, set with fine linens and lovely china, accented with crystal vases of fresh flowers are all appropriate touches for an Agwe fet. Even in Haiti, they make an extra effort to have the best of everything for this Man of the Sea.

You can make a feast for Agwe by offering any of the following items: champagne or white wine, champagne kola, and coffee with both sugar and cream. Sweet oils such as olive or almond, cane syrup, and such "white" foods as melon, rice cooked in coconut milk, rice cooked with lima beans (*pwa souche*), boiled or fried ripe banana (the small sweet yellow kind), and cake. His food offerings should always be placed on white chinaware, drinks served in nice glassware and coffee in china cups. Linens should be freshly laundered and starched, plates and glass immaculate, silverware shining. And preferably, this feast is done seaside.

Agwe is seen as a man of the world, refined and educated by all his travels. He is very experienced and knowledgeable, so his fets reflect this worldly outlook on life. He also enjoys some of the same offerings as his wife such as colognes and mirrors. Naval uniforms, nautical medals, rowing oars, and model boats/ships (or the real ones, if you have the space and money to do so!) His altars are decorated with items reflecting his sea life as well as his world travels. Set his space with any of the previously mentioned items as well as spyglasses, gyroscopes, astrolabes, glass floats and trinkets reflecting the world of seaports.

LaSiren / LaBalen: Sisters of the Deep

I love the ocean. I grew up on the shore of Connecticut where I was as much a seal as I was a kid. I could swim practically before I could walk -- a life saving teaching seaside communities give their children. I spent hours collecting seashells, swimming and watching out for the mermaids and mermen I was sure inhabited the coastal waters by my home. To this day, I enjoy nothing more than sitting on the beach and studying the waves.

I think that love of the ocean and beach translated into my love of Vodou when I found that the mermaid I sought as a kid, was here in the faith that I serve. LaSiren is envisioned as a beautiful dark haired woman with a fish tail on the lower half of her body - the classic mermaid. We sing this song to her in service:

LaSiren, La Balen, chapeau tombe nan la mer!

LaSiren, La Balen, my hat falls into the sea

Hats falling into the sea is a coded description for going under possession. Your head "falls" into unconsciousness, a metaphorical 'sea', where all the knowledge and power of the world preside. In that 'sea' is where we meet LaSiren, wife of Agwe Tawayo, the supreme Lwa of the ocean.

LaSiren is feminine, enchanting and sensual. She moves with unerring grace through the watery domain of her husband Agwe. She carries her trumpet, which she uses to call the faithful to service, seducing us with her siren song, taking our heads as it were, under the sea to gain "konnesans" - consciousness of the intuitive world.

LaSiren is considered to be the "Mother of the Fish." She shares this title with Yemaya of Santeria, whose names also mean "Mother whose Children are the Fish." In both cases, the inner meaning is that since she is the mother of the world, her children are too numerous to count - not unlike the fish who inhabit her domain of the sea.

Modern science has shown that life actually began in the oceans of the world. And, as a foetus, we swim for nine months in our mother's belly. So the stretch to calling the Ocean our Mother is not all that big - a large body of salt water, rolling and moving with the tides is not unlike being rocked in the womb of our mother. And just as early life evolved out of the oceans, we evolve from little fish-like foetuses into human beings at birth. We come from the waters and manifest ourselves into the reality of our world. This can be seen as an allegory of LaSiren, who brings her initiates knowledge from beneath her watery domain, helping them manifest their desires.

LaSiren is very beautiful as well as very powerful. It is said that if you fall under her spell, she will steal you away to her underwater kingdom. Here, she will keep you for a time (some stories say seven days, other say seven years). When you return, you will have the ability to perform feats of magic and divination. It is said those who have spent time in her watery domain return lighter in color, because they have gone beneath the waters.

There is no definitive root to trace for LaSiren in Haiti. Most likely (and this is my own conjecture, nothing more) LaSiren came from the Mami Wata complex of spirits. Mami Wata loosely translates as "Mother of the Waters" and is the name of a group of practices in Dahomey. These practices praise and serve a collection of waters spirits who all share similar organs in both legend and locations. Some are like Agbe and Naente, are said to be rulers of the ocean. Others hail from the Aziri river basin in Africa, a possible root for Erzulie. I have been taught that LaSiren belongs to this group, making her sister to Erzulie, as wells as Filomen and Dayila. Although her origins may be shrouded in mystery, LaSiren remains a very popular Lwa both in imagery and in sosyetes through Haiti.

Metaphysically, LaSiren represents the ability to nurture and nourish yourself, to replenish your energies and to take time out for yourself. Her ceaseless motion of waves and tides lends you endless energy. This can be a boon as well as a burden, because others may see you as someone who can perform miracles. If you are hearing the siren call of LaSiren, stop and ask yourself this - who or what is taking all your time and energy? Whose problems are you trying to fix at the expense of your own vital energy? And why are you trying to fix them? LaSiren is calling to you, to remind you that you are in charge of your own destiny, not the destiny of others. She is inviting you to take the plunge into her cool blue depths, to find the answers within yourself. But that can only be accomplished if you are willing to let go of the mundane world around you and plumb your own inner seas of unconsciousness and talents. LaSiren invites us to dance with her in an endless round of ebb and flow, the give and take of life.

LaSiren has a counterpart, called LaBalen. This is the dark, intuitive sister who swims below LaSiren's lighter blue domain. LaBalen is dark only in that she is the deep, deep depths of the world's oceans - she is our Shadow side, our inner intuition that we so seldom listen to. LaBalen children seem to float along as their Siren sisters do, but do not cross a LaBalen for any reason. LaBalen lends her children strong wills, determination and grit. No dilly-dallying with a LaBalen child!

There has been much written about fets for LaSiren. Like all marine Lwa, her services have a certain allure when performed at the beach, near the water. But it is not a necessity and she is certainly served just as well in an apartment altar space as she is by the beach. Just remember she is a "white" Lwa, meaning she is part of the cooler, older Rada pantheon. As such, she doesn't take sacrifices that involve blood (meaning live animals), a key point often over looked in all the writings about her and her sister LaBalen the whale.

Along with not receiving live animals , LaSiren rarely eats any real food, though some houses do serve her sweet pastries and light finger foods of that nature. Some houses serve her fish or shell fish, both raw or pan seared. She much prefers Champagne, perfume and her toiletries just like her sister Erzulie Freda does.

In possession states, LaSiren does not stand. She is a mermaid, with a fish tail, so the hounsi will spread a white or blue cloth for her to lay or "swim" upon. The LaSiren who comes here does sit up and loves champagne. She wants to be misted with perfume or water, and then gestures for her mirror and brush. She will brush her hair and gaze lovingly at everyone. Sometimes, she calls for shells and plays with them, other times she finds any water present and dunks herself into it. Her chwal has learned to bring dry clothing with her to services for her Mama.

LaSiren loves anything from the sea (obviously) including strings of pearls, seashells in different colors and coral of all kinds. She also will accept a mirror, perfume, a brush and her horn which she uses to call her servitors to her side. Serve her white foods such as iced cakes, finger size pastries, white cookies, white champagne and white wine. She is syncretized with the Diosa del Mar, or the Stella Maris, and her feast day coincides with the Catholic one on August 18th. Images of mermaids are also very popular and make a good centerpiece for her altars. Blue flowers, blue candles and perfume are all acceptable offerings.

Erzulie Freda: The Weeping Madonna

Maitresse Mambo Erzulie Freda Dahomey is the full and proper way to address this magnificent spirit. She is one of the best known of the Vodou Lwa and one of the most difficult to understand. Freda is powerful and beneficial as well as terrifying and demanding. Vodou does not have a woman as a goddess of fertility. Fertility is regarded as a unified principle, equally held by male and female forces. Danbala is united to his Ayida. Agwe Tawayohas his counterpart in LaSiren; the Marassa are seen as the paired forces of nature.

Erzulie is unique because she is represented in almost every nation of spirits as a solo Lwa. All alone, her energy is the solo pursuit of that which is unattainable. Without a partner to help her face the challenge, she always dissolves into tears at the perceived slight of her situation.

Erzulie can possibly be traced back to the West African Aziri river basin. Her name Erzulie is actually her surname, the one shared by all the sisters of this large group of Lwa. In the African style of names, her surname, "Erzulie" or sometimes said as "Ezili." The group then splits into the various Lwa that share similar traits.

Many of the Erzulie spirits are difficult to distinguish by character rather than the details of the nation in which they are served. Erzulie Boumba is represented in the Boumba group which is a Kongo nation. This Lwa is similar to Pomba Gira, the brash street walker in Candomble in Brazil. There is an Erzulie Seneka, Erzulie Doba, Erzulie Sibrakon, Erzulie Wango, Erzulie Mapyan (who is part of the Guédé escort), Ezili Je Wouj and many others too numerous to mention.

Erzulie is distinct from the other Lwa in many ways. Some Lwa represent the more metaphysical arenas of the world. For instance, Legba represents our ability to understand and make choices. Guédé represents our inevitable Death. Some Lwa represent natural phenomena like Sobo does for Storms, or Agwe does for the seas.

Other Lwa have a more grounded presence in the world – they interact with men on a more intimate and personal level. If we are a diverse lot, then the Lwa are a reflection of our own mixtures of characters, personalities and attitudes. They use their diverse energies to bring resolution to the requests made of them. Ogoun is a good example – his many avatars cover the gamut of responsibilities from military strategists to simple working men. Erzulie also falls into this social energy matrix.

Erzulie is not a Lwa of elemental forces, but THE Lwa of ideal dreams, hopes and aspirations. She is known as the earth mother, the goddess of love and avenger of wrongs to both women and men. Although she has no specific function, she is approachable in a confidential manner. Think of her as your wise and capable older sister.

Many people believe that Erzulie represents simple love. That is a gross over simplification of what is really a very complicated spiritual energy. Erzulie represents Perfection in the world. But we know the world is less than perfect.

Perfection has its darker side. The hunt for Perfection can degenerate into compulsion, obsession, or delusion. This bi-polar analogy is the place that Erzulie straddles. Her ability to maintain her balance comes directly from her gift of Love. If we agree that Love is the highest creative force in the universe, then one can fairly say that Erzulie Freda represents love at that level –- the love that brings everything into manifestation.

But Haiti is a tough country, and the people of Haiti struggle to survive with the meagerest of things. It is through that cultural lens that we see Erzulie stuck at the lower level of "love". This love is concerned with physical comforts (or lack thereof) that the average Haitian desires. Erzulie is a higher functioning energy, but she is often set too low in our expectations. We spend too much time asking her for the material gains of the world, when she is capable of giving so much more that mere objects. It is this dichotomy of extremes that fractures the energy of Erzulie into her pantheon of avatars.

For example, let's look briefly at Dantor and Freda. Both are in classic opposition because they represent two extremes of the Erzulie energy. However, they both belong to the same category or idea. For some people, the lap of luxury and adoration is ideal (Freda). Others would prefer active service (Dantor). This is the same energy, simply expressed in a different way.

Freda is most popular of the Erzulie sisters, but there are many others who hold important roles in Vodou. There is the refined Erzulie Gretor, who is similar to Freda though less given to extravagance and extremes of emotion. Gran-n Erzulie Kokobe (the shriveled) is an older spirit who appears as an arthritic old woman. Erzulie Kawoulo is associated with storms. Erzulie Boumba is prone to abusive language and lascivious behavior. Erzulie Doba is the grand dame of the Erzulie clan. Envisioned as a wealthy patroness, Doba is often described as a Main Line hostess, but not "old" in the chronological sense.

There is even an Erzulie who is a part of the Guédé family. Erzulie Ke Nwa (Erzulie of the Black Heart) walks with Guédé. And as previously mentioned, Erzulie Je Wouj is the height of Erzulie's rage at everything. And finally, the other popular Lwa of this family is Erzulie Dantor, who I will cover more extensively in the Petro section of this chapter.

Erzulie has no specific mate, although she is often placed with Danbala, Ogoun and Agwe as husbands. But in the truest sense, Erzulie is alone, as all powerful women must be. Houngan Max Beauvoir says "Erzulie is the female energy of Legba." (Max Beauvoir, 1990), seeing Legba as the primal male force of creative fire, his compliment then would be Erzulie, as the primal Female force of water.

Erzulie is also seen as purity. It is said that no poison, malefic magic or curses can exist in her presence. She is purity and light, negating these illnesses by her mere being. This is also one of the reasons she demands cleanliness and light from her servitors. Basil is one of her favorite scents, and servitors of Erzulie would do well to grow it abundantly on their property, strewing the fresh herb in their homes and making washes by soaking the leaves in water. Sprinkled throughout the home, the scented water lends Freda's blessing to your hearth.

Erzulie Freda has tremendous power and is feared as much as she is loved. She has several different roles: she is the Lwa of the word (and again, we see the relationship to Legba here), love, help, goodwill, health, beauty and fortune, as well as being the Lwa of jealousy, vengeance, and discord. She is sometimes referred to as a serpent that is coiled upon itself, living on water and bananas. Here we see her earlier connection to her African origins, where she was a spirit of the River Aziri; and the bananas that came to be fried in cinnamon and sugar for her to eat.

Vodou has a very special place for Erzulie because she is so uniquely human. She is the differentiating force between mankind and all other creation. Erzulie is the ability to conceptualize, the ability to dream, the artistic ability to create. Erzulie is often referred to as white or pale skinned. There are songs that sing of her pale color:

Ezili Fre, li fre, li yon bel fanm
Ezili Fre, li fre, li yon fanm blanch
Ezili O! Li pa manje moun anko
Inosan Bondye va gade ou

Erzulie is fresh, she is cool, she is a beautiful woman,
Erzulie is fresh, she is cool, she is a white woman,
Erzulie oh! She doesn't eat people any more,

God will consider you innocent.

I think this whiteness might also refer to her possible position in the Qabbala. Qabalistically speaking, she is Yesod, the female prototype of Vodou who represents the moon for dreams of promises as yet unfulfilled. In every temple there is a space dedicated just to her. This space is kept clean, perfumed and stocked with the very best items the servitor can afford for Erzulie. Her clothing is often kept freshly laundered or even dry cleaned in plastic covering, so that it is as clean as possible for her. Her toiletry items are always new and never previously used. At a recent fet for her, she cried inconsolably when she realized that the perfume had just been sprayed. (I had used her Anais-Anais to call her down on her chwal.) The very act of bringing her down also caused her to chastise me for my use of her very personal things!

Cleanliness is paramount to Erzulie, as she must distance herself from the rest of the world through her overt mannerisms and cleanliness. She will demand that the room be sprinkled with perfume or perfumed water, to cool it down and freshen it. She will often douse all present with perfume as well, to sweeten the room to her preference. We have had to lay down fresh sheets for her to place her foot upon or clean the altar in her presence, because she was not happy with the way things appeared.

Erzulie Freda is fond of sweet alcohols, elaborately decorated pastries and dainty finger foods. She has been compared to Aphrodite, a libertine who loves many men and ignores women. Pleasure loving as well as extravagant, Erzulie loves to receive gifts as well as bestow them. When offered a cake at one of her parties, she spent a good amount of time careful slicing and doling out dainty pieces to all the men.

Freda loves men, and will demonstrate the true art of coquetry. Batting her lashes, she will kiss and hug all the men present, dancing with them, offering pieces of her foodstuff and sharing sips of pink champagne. However, if there are women present, she barely acknowledges them. She will respond to her own female servitors, but will simply offer them a pinky of her hand. Haughty, proud and stand-offish, she will respond only in French to those she deems less than important. But to the men, she will fawn and flirt all night long. And yet, she is closely associated with the Blessed Virgin Mary and her symbol is the heart, usually one broken with an arrow.

Erzulie wears three wedding bands since she has been (or is) married to Danbala, Ogoun and Agwe. She has often flirted with Azaka, but she has dismissed Guédé as unworthy, due to his coarse language and obscene gestures.

A visit from Erzulie is never fully satisfying to the Lwa. In the end she always begins to weep. The party is not fun enough, the food is not fresh enough, there was not enough champagne. The potential of the event has not fulfilled her desire. And so her tears flow, and people rush to try and make her smile. She is, in the end, the one who suffers the burdens of the world.

Despite her flirtations and loving ways, Erzulie is a virgin in the manner that her womb has not been opened by childbirth. . In her placement in the Priye Ginen, she falls Qabalistically in Yesod, the sphere of the Moon. Sitting between the realm of the divine and the realm of men, she is caught between that which is and that which can be. Divorced from the Godhead, unable to move up or down, she weeps for her loss of contact with Divine and the inability to fully manifest her desires in mankind. A pivotal placement, for she is part of both and fully of neither one.

Her origins are in the sea making intuition, psychic abilities and dreams part of her metaphysical energies. At one time, she shared this role with Gran Simba, LaSiren and LaBalen, but has become completely divorced from her watery origins. She is now seen almost exclusively as a personification of feminine grace and beauty. It is no wonder that she weeps, separated as she is from all that she loves.

Freda's colors are pink and white, or pale blue and white. Serve her foods on crystal or white china dishes. Everything should be as elaborate as you can afford to make it. She loves pink, so give her pink or white roses, lacey hankies to dab at her weeping eyes, sweet pastries such as petit fours, cakes with white and pink icing, white sweet puddings, rice boiled in milk with a little white sugar added, fried mangos and plantains rolled in sugar or honey (with or without cinnamon).

She will also accept Pink Champagne and clear Creme de Menthe as drinks. Her favorite perfume is Anais-Anais by

Chaparelle, but she will also accept Pompeii Lotion, Champagne de Ball, Ysatis de Givenchy, Orange Flower Water or Rose Water.

She loves Ultra-Light Virginia Slims Menthol Cigarettes, fancy soaps in pretty wrappers, new money and any kind of jewelry, but especially ropes of pearls and gold chains. Some servitors keep three rings for her, representing her three husbands. We have a gold snake ring for Danbala, a gold dolphin ring for Agwe and a silver band for Ogoun on her altar.

Freda's service days are Tuesdays and Thursday. Her vèvè is a checkered heart with the letter "M" through the middle. She is syncretized with the Mater Dolorosa de Monte Cavario (Our Lady of Mount Calvary) for all the gold jewellery and chains draped on the image of the Virgin. Freda feast day is September 15 as is the Mater Dolorosa's.

~~~

These then are the main Rada Lwa that we serve in our sosyete. There are hundreds of other Rada spirits served all over Haiti and in the Diaspora. Their services, songs and servitors reflect the ever changing and evolving face of Vodou today. And new spirits continue to come forward as new comers enter the faith, and new cultures touch upon the realms of the Lwa. This is all expected and good. A living faith that keeps up with its servitors is more than likely to find new energies, new ideas and new paradigms to work with. A faith that can embrace all the diversity of its congregations will always be on the vanguard of belief. The inclusive nature of Vodou realizes its apotheosis of religious practice, by doing just that: by embracing all the people who come to it, ensuring its presence and practice for all future generations.

Chapter Seven: The Petro Nation

In the Priye Djo, the Rada segment is followed by the Nago nation who herald the start of the Petro listing of spirits. The Ogouns that serve in Agwe's fleet are named here: Ogoun Badagris, Ogoun Balendjo, Ogoun Ossange. The Nago nation also serves as the entry point for the Djouba nation, who's favorite son is Azaka and for the Adja nation, with the naming of Bossou as we transition into this portion of service. These last names of the smaller city states within the larger one of Dahomey are the transition between the older African modes of worship and the modern styles that came about on the island Haiti.

Petro services are considered more intense. The Lwa honored here originate both in Africa and in the New World. A very few others who don't fit logically elsewhere (meaning, we don't know their origin), are called and honored here as well. Petro rites take many ceremonial details from Kongo and West African rites such as the Oro society and the Zangbeto[33]. There are also many native American (Arawak, Taino, Carib) elements.

Petro rites and its Lwa are considered "Hot". This means they are easily agitated, quicker to action and in some cases, are more dangerous to deal with regarding magical work and outcomes. Maya Deren said it well: " As the Haitians put it, the Petro are "*plus raide*" - more hard, more tough, more stern, less tolerant and forgiving, more practical and demanding. If

[33] Davis, C.B. (2008). *The African Diaspora Encyclopedia*. Santa Barbra, CA: ABC-CLIO, Inc..Vol 1

the Rada represent the protective, guardian powers, the Petro Lwa are the patrons of aggressive action."[34]   They are fiery in all aspects of their services, from music to dance to even their foods. Meal offerings are cooked differently than Rada spirits, with fire grilling being a preferred method. Petro spirits drink their kleren and rum spiked with habanera peppers and other hot tasting spices.   Petro dances are defiance in action with fists clenched, feet kicking and performed in group formations.

The Petro nations include Nago, Kongo, Gola (Angolan), and Kreyol (Haitian). Karen Brown described these Lwa as military or foreigners. And indeed, given the large Ogoun group, one can easily see this distinction here. Petro is where we find the African Ogoun re-imagined as the Haitian Ogoun Feray, Batala, Shango and Des Manieres.

I have always said that for an island nation, they love their military men. The idea of military is directly related to the necessity of survival in Haiti. Brown has talked about the selective needs of the slaves in the New World. Their immediate survival depended upon their ability to fight – for their food or their lives. This necessity of survival naturally led to a rise in the service of military spirits such as Ogoun.

In Africa, Ogoun's associations included blacksmithing as well as the role of protector of hunters and clearer of forest paths. These are barely detectable in his avatar in Haiti. In Haiti, his connection to soldiering was the one the slaves needed the most, hence his nearly autonomous role as a military strategist and fighting warrior.

---

[34] Deren, M. (1953). *The Divine Horsemen: Living Gods of Haiti*. London and New York: Thames and Hudson.

This idea of military Lwa is not relegated solely to the Nago nation, though they surely are the dominant group. There are military spirits in the Kongo grouping as well. Liza McAlister mentions Simbi Gangan as a militarized "Kongo" Lwa, who comes as a commander in chief and orders everyone around the temple.[35]

This brings to mind what military means in Haiti and how it translates to the Vodou Lwa. Some of the Lwa are obviously military, as in the Nago nation and the previously mentioned Kongo. But others wear their military mystique in their bearing or in a love for fire, fireworks and gun powder. Kafou for instances will come into possession with an upright posture, his arms held rigidly out, spread as if attached to a cross. He struts stiffly, reminiscent of the goose stepping military of World War II Germany. Don Petro and Gross Point love fire and I have seen their vèvès drawn with gunpowder, then lit and fired off. And finally when Mambo Dantor arrives in service at this house, she wants fireworks, sparklers and her blade dipped in florida water, then lit up for her pleasure.

Petro is not a nation, but a style of service under which many African nations are served. As I mentioned, Kongo, Nago, Zoklimo, Senegal and Wangolo are a few of the many groupings that fall under this category. The New World Lwa come under this heading: Mambo Erzulie Danto, with her blades and scars; Don Petro who was thought to be a Spanish slave and his son Ti-Jean Petro (not to be confused with Danto's son of the same name). The Caciques (chiefs of the Arawaks) fall under this grouping as

---

[35] McAlister, L. (2002). *Rara! Vodou, Power and Performance in Haiti.* Berkeley: University of California Press.

well as those remnants of Native American legends and peoples that are still held in distant memory.

At the dawn of the plantocracy, there were still Natives living in the mountain regions of the islands. The maroon or runaway Africans were taken in by these people, intermarried with them and brought their bloodlines into the mix of the islanders as well as their own African lineages. These Native Ancestors are no longer spoken of by the newer sosyetes, but the old places like Soukri and Souvenance name Lwa that have no African ancestry, but are still a part of the ancestral heritage sung for in the Priye Ginen at large services such as the Easter week ceremonies at the lakou in Souvenance.

The Petro Lwa retain some of their slavery attributes: the Lwa Ti Jean Petro plays with fire, demonstrating his invincibility to the flames. This is a remnant of field punishment. Slaves were branded with irons or punished by being rolled into a bundle of burning sugar cane. The Lwa Maynette comes with broken hands and feet, a show of the punishment meted out for her participation in the Bois Caiman rite.

There are an entirely different set of tools used in Petro, with regard to the Lwa. Rada rites with their smooth rhythms and rolling drum beats need nothing more than water and songs to call up the spirits. Petro rites with their broken rhythms, sharp drum beats and staccato footsteps require more than songs to call down the energy of the night.

Military uniforms, field whips, whistles and the clang of iron are all remnants of slavery times, and have their place in Petro services. One of the favored methods of calling the Lwa in the Petro rites is to use a whip made from jute and snapped with gusto at the important places throughout the peristyle. Some of the Lwa love metal police whistles and will commandeer the whistle to use as their voice. And finally, the shackles of slavery are remembered in the clang of the iron bell and the rings of iron on the drums, beaten in syncopation for the Spirits.

Red is the preferred color of the Petro nations. Most spirits have a second color added, to help distinguish them from one another. The favored color combinations are blue with red or black with red. Though various Lwa from different parts of the country are served with a variety of colors and patterns, red is always the dominant color.

Legba Petro: The Guardian of the Inner Crossroads

Legba Petro is the fiery aspect of the Lwa Legba, served Petro style. Although he is seen as a separate entity from Legba in Rada, he is another ray off the same energy vibe. Or, to use the imagery of a gemstone, he is another facet of the Legba diamond.

Legba Petro reclaims the solar aspect of Legba from Africa and focuses it through the lens of a Petro service. Metaphysically speaking, Legba Petro is a potent and dynamic energy that inspires people to great heights of creation, imagination and possibilities. Author and magician Louis Martinie likens this Legba to the Pure Fool or the Enlightened Fool, the difference between them a subtle but important one.

The Pure Fool can create monumental works, but they have no lasting effect. Think beautiful ice sculptures that melt away or a fireworks display that awes the viewer for a moment, but then burns out immediately.

The Enlightened Fool also creates exceptional things, but the work is much more likely to persist over time.[36] Mozart's talent for creating gorgeous music is a good example. Defying the norms of the Viennese musical school, he chose to light up the stage with operas that no one had ever seen before or since. And they are still here for us to enjoy.

Both reflect Petro Legba's influences. As the Pure Fool, he encourages us to foolish choices, made in an instant of desire or gratification. As the Enlightened Fool, he inspires us to greatness, helping us achieve monumental goals with seeming ease. Both are Legba Petro demonstrating his great talent for encouraging us to step off the proverbial cliff, to give it a try (whatever 'it' may be.).

We sing this song to Legba at the beginning of a Petro rite:

Salwye Legba, eh! Legba nan Petro, salwye Legba, e!

Legba e, Legba nan Petro, salwye Legba, e!

Si nou tout te konnen, Nou tout t'ap fe pou ko nou

Salute, Legba, eh! Legba in Petro, salute Lega e!

Legba, e, Legba in Petro, salute Legba, e!

If you all know how, you all would do it for yourselves

The allusion to doing it yourself is an inner reflection on the work of Petro, which is secret and often hidden in both meaning and metaphor. The Petro side is the island side of Vodou. Here is where the Africans "hid"

---

[36] Martinie, L. & Glassman, S. (1996) *The New Orleans Voodoo Tarot.* Stamford, CT: U.S. Games Systems, Inc.

what they were doing from the masters. Here is where they hid, literally from sight, so that they could work in private.

Legba Petro's work is often hidden and hard to conceive. We sing to help draw Him out so He will open the gates to the Petro world, allowing the Lwa to come down to be with the congregation.

The Petro nation is a power house of energies that contain such luminaries as Gran Bwa, Simbi Makaya and Gran Simba. Only an equally powerful gatekeeper could be the force behind which these energies gather for entrance into the world of men.

Martinie says Legba Petro walks on points of fire, and I think that is an accurate description. When this Legba descends into service, he walks firmly upright with an intense stare at the congregation. Legba Petro loves cigars, hot spiced rum and heavily seasoned meats. He will also accept cakes with red icing and red wine with spices.

Legba Petro is often syncretized with Saint Anthony of Padua, for his youthful appearance as well as his ability to find lost items. This search function is a very useful tool for the Lwa to have. Lost things often include lost lovers, lost money and lost chances. Legba Petro restores all of these and much more.

Marassa Petro: The Fiery Triplets of Petro

Next in Petro service, following Legba are the Marassa. And again, when we speak of Marassa Petro, we are speaking about the Marassa, served Petro Style. Where in the Rada side of services, they are envisioned as the cosmic duality of the Saints Cosmos and Damien, here they are seen as the trinity of Faith, Hope and Charity. Their chromolithograph shows three very pretty girls, facing inward, with secret smiles on their faces.

But these are not fainting violets – oh no, these three spirits are tough as nails and will not bend for an instant. So capricious and quick to change their minds, their positions on work and their outcomes, they are feared by most Vodouisants. The saying goes you only serve the Marassa Petro, if you have triplets in your family or the spirits themselves call you to do work for Them.

In the Vodou theological construct of life, one plus one equals three. It is the idea of two things coming together and creating a higher note from the combined energies. We see this energy manifest in the world all the time. A musician and his instrument combine to make music. An artist and their medium, create artwork. Even on a mundane level, we combine into a trinity with each event that comes into contact with us. It is the one of the basic building blocks of the universe that brings harmony and balance by manifesting the energies of two into three. Two points define a line, but three define a plane. Marassa Petro combines to create multiple planes of existence in this reality that might otherwise go unnoticed.

The servitors of Haiti diffuse these Spirits into two distinct groupings. The first and more popular is the Marassa Kay, thought to be the Creole version of the Great Twins. These are the "sweeter" pair, who are fed within the peristyle proper, are propitiated through the feast known as *Manje Marassa*, and who confer great blessings to their servitors.

The second and lesser known pairing are the Marassa Ginen. These are the fierce Marassa who are considered to have been left behind in Africa, and are fed outside of the peristyle proper. They are further diffused into Marassa Kongo and Marassa Bwa, twins of the forests. They are fed on a three chambered wooden plate, with the third chamber attached at the intersection of the other two.

Anthropologist Harold Courlander characterizes the Marassa Bwa as "savage or untamed." Although this sounds like a harsh description for children, I think it is because the Marassa Bwa are connected to Gran Bwa, the spirit of the untamed forest. The Marassa are prohibited from being served leaves of any kind. This would make sense, as they are rulers of the leaves, and use them for healing purposes.

In Saint Marc, the Marassa are further delineated as Marassa Bwa Makak, taking their name form the creole word *makak*, after the monkey of the same name. They are served their offerings in large wooden trays that are placed in the branches of a tree near the houmfort, since the spirit of the Marassa Bwa Makak is considered to manifest itself in the monkeys that live in the trees, which is the domain of Gran Bwa. This is an interesting intersection of Lwa, symbols and meaning.

Author and art collector Marilyn Houlberg says the relationship between twins and monkeys in Vodou is comparable to the Yoruba notion of that twins are related to *edun*, the Colombus monkey, since monkeys and humans give birth to almost identical twosomes.[37]

However we see them, the Marassa Petro are a volatile spiritual trinity that require careful service. You do not casually serve the Marassa

---

[37] Houlberg, M. (2005) The ritual cosmos of the twins. In P. Bellegarde-Smith (Ed.), *Fragments of Bones: neo-African religions in a new world.* (pp.13-31). Urbana, IL: University of Illinois Press.

Petro. In fact, as I stated earlier, you should only serve Marassa Petro only if you are a triplet, have triplets in your family or are called to do so by the Lwa during a service. To begin serving these spirits and then stop for any reason is to bring their fierce and hot natures into play. That is something I would not recommend to anyone!

As I said previously, the image most often used to symbolize the Marassa Petro is the chromolithograph of the Three Virtues, for it includes the Dosu/Dosa, the child born following a twin birth. This child is seen as the most powerful of the three.

Depending on the nation of Marassa Petro, they are served in a specific manner. As previously mentioned, Marassa Petro eat outside the peristyle proper. They are served the same foods as their Rada counterparts. Appropriate meals would include child like foods that can be eaten with your fingers or hands. Red beans and rice, pudding, fried banana *peze* (chunks of banana fried in sugar), sweet sodas and cookies are all acceptable foods. Marassa Petro do not take their food spiced or heated -- these spirits are hot enough without adding any energy to their presence.

Marassa Petro adore toys, showing a preference for toys made from metal like jacks, a beach pail and shovel or trucks and cars to the softer items of their Rada cousins. As with their Rada counterparts, you must give them the exact same thing thrice (three of each thing), or risk them becoming jealous and not working with you. Like a child, they are capricious and can flare to anger quickly. But with a steady hand (just as with children), they respond with love, affection and attention.

Having twins in both our families, the Houngan and I serve the Marassa with great affection and delight. They make their presence known to us through numbers. Although we have often changed our phone, our number always has a double digit. Our bank accounts, the Houngan's security pins at the various corporate offices he has worked in, our mailing addresses, even the date of our anniversary (the 11th of June) are all reflections of the Marassa's presence in our lives. Just recently, we hosted a fet for the Marassa as a fund raiser for Haiti. We set the altar with our twin paraphernalia, we had exactly 22 people present and when I tallied up the money we garnered, it was $2,233.22. Thank you Marassa, for this wonderful example of your presence!

Ogoun Petro: The fiery warrior

Ogoun is part of the Nago Nation of spirits, those energies that came directly to the New World from West Africa. The Ogoun who crossed the Atlantic was a figure in the same classic tradition as the Greek Zeus. He was a sky divinity of the Nigerians, Lord of thunderbolt, fire and might. By logical extension, he was patron of warriors, and of the iron smiths, forgers of war weapons.[38]

Unlike some of the Lwa who split into separate entities upon arriving here (Hevesio who became Sobo, Bade and Agasou, for example), Ogoun retained much of his lore, attributes and talents. Vodou is a collective creation that does not exact the abandonment of one tribal deity for another. We see this clearly displayed in the attributes of Ogoun who is seen in Haiti as a military man. His attributes of blacksmithing and forestry

---

[38] Jennings, L. (2008). *Toni Morrison and the idea of Africa.* New York:Cambridge Press.

although less prominent in Haiti, are still similar to what they were in Africa. A bonfire called Ogoun's forge burns before every houmfort during the Kanzo cycle of services. Everyone who passes by the houmfort can see the blaze and knows that Ogoun is standing guard over the Kanzo.

Ogoun's love of fire is one attribute that correlates to astrology. The author Mercedes Foucard Guignard states that all Ogouns are Aries, another Mars ruled sign of the Zodiac. I think you could make the argument that Ogoun is a Mars ruled Lwa. Mars is the sign of war and strife; Ogoun is the Lwa of war and vengeance.

Mars also is one of the planets that rules Scorpio with Pluto being the other. Pluto is the Roman name for Hades, lord of the underworld. Iron and ore are from the underworld (earth); Ogoun rules iron and mineral ores. It is not a big stretch to see the connection here. Along with kanzo, Ogoun's forge is lit when an Ogoun service is being held. The bonfire is built around a bar of iron that is buried along with certain offerings. Four feet is left above ground. That exposed bar turns a brilliant red once the main fire gets going. Its glowing heat is a beacon in the night, letting people passing by know that Ogoun is in the temple and being served.

Martinie says you can hear Ogoun in the world around us. You can hear Him in the clang of machinery at a downtown construction site. He is the rattle of trains on tracks or the sound of a car's engine. All that metallic ringing is the sound of Ogoun's metaphysical forge, banging out into the night with Ogoun's energy and vibration. Ogoun is everywhere.

I have been asked if the Lwa ever increase in number. I do feel that where the Lwa are served privately, they increase as family members ascend to the status of Lwa. But the main stars of Vodou like Ogoun simply shift and evolved as their servitors needs evolve or the people themselves grow and change.

Ogoun is a chimera, forever changing and shifting. I think he assumes a new face, a new mask, to help him survive in the new places and countries he enters. There is no additional Ogoun. His energy matrix is large and sound. But he changes as we need him.

In Haiti, Ogoun had dozens of faces. Let is return to the diamond analogy again. Look at this diagram:

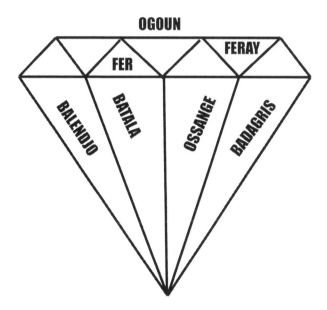

Each facet of the diamond is a different face of Ogoun, yet the entire diamond is also Ogoun. And as Ogoun moved into the new world, his facets changed to reflect the myriad scenarios in which he was needed:

He became the medical Ogoun - Ogoun Balendjo, ruling the metals of medicine - stethoscopes, needles, surgical knives, operating tables, gurneys, wheelchairs. He powers research and science through the metals of a medical laboratory. He finds new ways to seek out the enemy (disease) through MRIs, CAT scans and miniature cameras that go into the battlefield (the human body) and destroy the enemy. He is the laser that zaps cancer tumors and the mesh of a stent inserted into a blocked artery.

He became the modern Ogoun Des Manieres, Ogoun "two ways", associated with electronic metals that carry currents in two directions - circuitry boards, computers and extension cords, anything that conducts electric impulses.

He became Ogoun Shango, an important king in Africa known for his decision making and bravery in battle. He gives his knowledge of the forge and war to those who make decisions and fight a very different kind of battle – one of words in the courtroom, or at the negotiating table. I like to think of Ogoun Shango as the modern day Solomon, a figure my godmother revered in her Vodou work. She shared her visions with me of a king who uses his tongue as his sword, his wit as his rapier and his mind as a blade[39]. All of which speaks to Shango's love of weaponry and Ogoun's love of metal.

He is the father figure in Ogoun Batala, owning and ruling the metal of the body - brain impulses, heart beats, electrolytes. We don't think of the human body as having metal, but the fact is that we carry iron to make hemoglobin, along with a host of mineral salts like copper, sodium potassium, calcium, magnesium and others. All these are needed for our "electric systems" to function correctly.

---

[39] *Conversation with Mambo Shakmah Winddrum, 2003*

I am fascinated by Ogoun, because he is an excellent example of my Nephilim theory in practice. In occult esoteric studies, Nephilim are the result of a divine/human mating. If the gods did indeed mate with us, and left behind progeny to help us, then Ogoun is one of those Demi-divine beings who is still making himself known to us through his many avatars and attributes. In fact, he is the best example of the phrase, "They wear the mask we are most likely to accept." I do not believe it is in the Lwa nature to blow us away with a frightening visage, gross smells and strange sounds. I honestly believe the Lwa want to communicate with us.

Ogoun is very good example. He continues to evolve along with us. We no longer use a forge to make iron weapons. We use a computer to fight our battles. He works with us through the circuitry and electronic impulses of the machine. We use his metals in machinery for farming, oil drilling and construction work. He evolves with us, helping us find new metals, new ideas and new methods of employing his amazing genius.

Ogoun has even gone where no Lwa has gone before – into outer space. Think not? Every rocket that powers up and launches, is ridden by Ogoun. The metal of the scaffolding, the rocket itself, all the circuit boards, electronic wiring and metal snaps, hooks and closures on the astronaut's suit, every bit of it is ruled by Ogoun. He has gone to the moon and back, in our space ships. Remember Apollo 13? Those men should not have been able to come home. But Ogoun prevailed, helping them find new ways to use the metal on board the orbiter. The Jet Propulsion Labs were using computers we tossed out 10 years ago to do the math and figure out the fuel equations; Ogoun helped the scientist on the ground compute the equations needed to bring those men home. The astronauts scoured the orbiter for anything they could use to retro fit their space craft, to assure re-entry.

Ogoun was there. And the navy seals who dropped out of helicopters in the sky, to help retrieve those astronauts from the ocean? Ogouns as well, the so-called "wet ones" who serve on Agwe's fleet: Ogoun Ossange, Ogoun Badagris and Ogoun Balendjo.

Think of it this way - when we first took flight in a jet, it was Ogoun who rode along with the pilots - breaking the sound barrier, breaking the lock of gravity on a space ship. He has helped us figure out how to make lighter, stronger metals (aluminium, titanium, titanium aluminide), and how to better protect our armies and police (Kevlar vests). He is been there when we placed telescopes in space and nanobots in bodies. In a way, Ogoun is the most prolific of all the Lwa, for he is ever changing, ever evolving his skills and gifts, to better meet the needs of the world around him and his servitors.

When you hear about a new breakthrough in medical science, think of Ogoun - because you can be sure they used his weapons of microscopes, centrifuges and robotize arms to find it. When you see construction of a new, faster train, think of Ogoun - because it is running on his tracks of iron and using electronic energy to run the engine.

Offer him rum, a cigar and some metal to protect our boys and girls across the sea. For no matter how busy he gets with all his new technologies, ideas and inventions, he is first and foremost, a warrior. He will keep them safe, for they are truly his "chosen few". Long into the night, Ogoun rages on the battlefields of the world, fighting for all of us.

You may serve all the Ogouns with metal. Metal pots, iron cauldrons, enamel camping plates are all correct vessels in which to place his food offerings. All the Ogouns take a red cloth as their mushoir or head wrap. We have also used a Haitian flag mushoir on his altar and under his plates, as a cloth to serve him on. All the Ogouns receive red and navy blue as their colors, though some do have a specific coloration.

Ogoun Batala receives white with gold braid. And Ogoun Shango also loves gold braid on his navy blue and red fabrics. But my favorite avatar of this magnificent Lwa is Ogoun Ossange.

Ossange is a retired warrior. It is said that Ossange is Danbala's priest and it is he who holds the tongue of Danbala – in other words, the asson and its flickering braid at the head of the gourd. This is also a reference to his ability to speak for Danbala who does not. Ossange's colors are the blue and azure green of the ocean. He is further dressed in a red cape with braid on the shoulder, signifying his special status as a member of Agwe's wayfaring Nago sailors.

Those sailors include Ogoun Balendjo, the Lwa who rules medical metals. This avatar has taken the battle into the operating room, where he heals with metal. Along with Ossange and Balendjo, Ogoun Badagris the third "wet" Ogoun of Agwe's fleet. He is envisioned as a secretary who keeps lists, writes laws into effect with metal tip pens and uses his warrior skills in the courtrooms and boardrooms of commerce.

Serve Ogoun on Wednesday by offering him rum, cigars and a machete. A true Renaissance Lwa, he is served in both the Rada and Petro rites. In the Rada rites, he is syncretized with Saint Jacques Majeur, the Spanish saint on a white horse. In the Petro rite, servitors use the image of Saint George slaying the dragon. Many houses use different saints for different avatars of Ogoun. I have seen Saint Michael, Saint Expedite and Saint Elias used, as well as Saint Joan of Arc. When in doubt, use the image of Saint Jacques. His is the most popular image, and the most profound in his mysteries. That is because of the black knight riding behind the saint, said to be Guédé collecting the dead off the battlefield.

Erzulie Dantor: The Black Madonna

Erzulie Dantor (pronounced DAN-tor) is one of the most popular and well served mysteries of the Vodou religion. She is the principle of motherhood, the strong and ferocious woman who works very hard for her family with little reward. She is associated with tough country ways and is fiercely independent. As a Petro Lwa, Erzulie Dantor is considered to be an extremely tough lady, and can be notoriously difficult to control.

Dantor is said to be "dumb", meaning silent. When in possession of her horse, the only sound emitted is a "ke-ke-ke-ke" stuttering. There are songs that say she had her tongue cut out. But I suggest that her inability to speak comes from her exhaustion and her fury at working so hard to feed her children and tend her land. It is the inevitable anger and frustration at having so little, despite great effort otherwise.

In the Haitian countryside, the women work from sun-up to sun-down and then some. Their men are often gone for the week, into the city to earn better wages. It is not uncommon in Haiti to find a single middle age woman, tilling land, washing clothes, preparing meals and tending small children and elderly parents. Along with all this "domestic" work, comes the harvesting and selling of goods to feed these people.

The country women walk long miles every day to the Carrefour (the crossroads), carrying their baskets of fruit, produce and herbs on their heads. They get up before sunrise, to make a meal for the family, before walking the long dirt roads, so they can get a good place in the market. After toiling in the sun all day, they then walk the miles home, not to rest, but to cook, clean and get ready for the next day's work.

At the end of this day when your child is crying and there is nothing for them to eat it is easy to just moan. You hurt from the labors of the day, but still have to go chop wood for the fire or haul water to make coffee. You can understand how someone would not be able to talk. It would take too much energy, too much effort. Better to just moan and point. The family will understand what you say, even if there are no words.

In the middle of the night, when you are feeling sick, but a parent is sicker and so you sit with them, you find yourself moving out of yourself, to feel the anger and frustration of the situation. That anger wells up and a thoughtform emerges, taking over, giving you the strength to carry on. Erzulie Dantor comes into manifestation out of the thoughts of all those market women, walking miles every day. Dantor rises from the rage of not being able to find a better job, a better house, a better school.

Dantor is like a Madansara – the tiny black birds of Haiti that are so noisy and busy in trees and rafters, building nests, tending their young, mating and fighting. They are the perfect symbol of Dantor and her energy. When Dantor comes in ritual, she is ready to work. She rolls up her sleeves and digs in. When offered her favorite sacrificial food, a female creole pig, she cuts off one ear and sucks the blood. Then, she gets busy sacrificing, butchering and cooking it for her children. Not one for shying away from the hard work, Dantor dives in with both hands to help her children.

Dantor also has a special place in Kanzo – for the tying of things is her specialty. It is not uncommon for us to find Dantor manifesting at one of our annual Pile Fey, taking over the herbs, encouraging us to work harder, faster and put more of ourselves into the work. Dantor, with her holy sweat, pours her love and devotion into the powdered herbs, blessing and consecrating them.

These same herbs she sometimes then ties up into special little bundles called pakets. During the Kanzo cycle, when pakets are made, it is Dantor who is often called into the djevo, to lend her energy and her ashe to the work. The following song is especially important to the kanzo cycle, because of the final line:

Erzulie fanm Ti-Jean metres kay-la,

Pa rele, se ou pote Houngan nivo,

Pa rele, so ou pote wanga pi fo,

Erzulie fanm Ti-Jean metres kay la,

Paket mwen a tout mare.

Erzulie Ti-Jean is woman, mistress of the house,

Don't cry out, it is you who carries the new Houngan,

Don't cry out, it is you who carries the strongest spells,

Erzulie Ti-Jean is woman, mistress of the house,

My paket is all tied up.

Dantor may be a country woman, but she knows her magic. She is married to three powerful Petro Lwa – Ogoun Feray, Ti-Jean Petro and Simbi Makaya. But as in all magical marriages, there are struggles.

Ogoun Feray is also married to her sister Freda, and so must split his time between the rivals. Ti-jean is also said to be Dantor's son and in a mystical arrangement, also her Twin Brother. Simbi Makaya is a very powerful magician. Patron of the secret society known as Sanpwel (nightwalkers), he is often gone, leaving her to fend for herself.

It is Ogoun who taught her the magic of the forge and the forest, both his domains. Ti-Jean knows many magical formulas and is thought to be a remnant of Taino Indian myths. And of course, Makaya (who is very name means Simbi of the leaves), has given her his knowledge of poison and cures. Dantor may not speak in words, but her language is the one spoken in the occult world of the magic of the forge, of forest and leaves, fire and spirits. Such power was prevalent in the stories of the revolution, particularly of that fateful night in the woods at Bwa Kayiman.

Many of the stories about the actions of the Bwa Kayiman ceremony, which began the Haitian Revolution, say that Erzulie Dantor was the Lwa who rode in the head of the presiding mambo, Cecil Fatima. One story says that the declaration was written in the blood of the sacrificed pig, on the skin of a White French man. There is no scholarship to prove such a point, but the story is startling for its intensity. The significance of Bwa Kayiman is one possible link to the service of Dantor on the 15th of August

Dantor was said to ride in the head of the Africans as they fought for their freedom. I would suggest that this was the manifestation known as Erzulie Je-Wouge, the most violent of the Dantor avatars. She rages, destroying everything in her path. However, in the end, her rage turns inward, destroying herself in the process:

Set kout kouto, set kout pwenya,

Prete m dedin a pou m al vomi sang mwen,

Sang mwen ape koule

Seven stabs of the knife, Seven stabs of the point,

Hand me a basin for I am going to vomit blood!

My blood is flowing!

I have been asked about this song, and what it means. Does Dantor really vomit blood in possession? But I think it is deeply tied to the revolution. The seven stabs of the knife is a metaphysically formula. Seven in metaphysics means completion. But more importantly, I think it means 'you (the perpetrator) can stab me as much as you want. I will not give you the secrets. All you will receive is my blood.' The people who fought in the revolution knew that their lives might be taken. But the reward of freedom was too great a cause to give up on. So they would choose to be tortured (seven stabs of the knife), but instead of information, all the torturer would get is blood. To me this song represents not only the bravery of Dantor in the revolution, but her willingness and determination not to give away anything. She would give her life first, so that others would continue to live to fight for freedom.

Possessions by Dantor tend to be very moving affairs. She cannot speak, but utters the staccato 'ke-ke-ke-ke' all the while gesturing to make herself understood. She hugs her children, tenderly washing faces, heads and hands. She will always serve her children food first, hand feeding them, making sure they have food and drink – refusing anything until all her children are cared for. She will make bathes and cleanse her initiates. She often washes the presiding Houngan or Mambo, recharging their pwen and pakets from their couche.

Seeing Dantor in action is to witness the Mother of the World in motion. By caring so deeply for us, we are offered salvation by her presence, her gestures, her work and her body. Born in anger, she resolves to work hard, so that the anger is transformed into blessings.

Though served in the Petro rites, her origin, like all Lwa bearing the name Erzulie, is from the Aziri river basin in West Africa. Some people claim her origins in the traditions of the Native Taino. Houngan Aboudja (Ronald Derencourt) has said that there is a Dantor served at Souvenance called Erzulie Dantor Daome who wears pink and blue denim and appears to be somewhat an amalgamation of the two. This is interesting to me personally, as Souvenance is an old line Rada house (the oldest as a matter of fact) and generally does not honor Kongo or Petro Lwa.

Dantor is deeply honored in the island's Northern areas, the ancestral home of the Kongo nation. She is known there as Zila Moyo. In the Northwest, she is Manzila Manyan. At Soukri, she is Madanm Lenmba. In the South, they call her Mambo Zila. In the West near Port-au-Prince, they use the name Erzulie Dantor. And everywhere she is known as La Reine Kongo.

The feud between Erzulie Dantor and her sister Erzulie Freda Dahomey is legendary but the real enemy of Dantor is Erzulie Mapyan, "she who lies". Here is a story from Mercedes Foucard Guignard's *Descent of the*

Lwa, regarding the reason behind the scars on Dantor is face. The translation is my own:

"It was during the battle of Bwa Kayiman, when the great revolutionary force summoned the adepts who controlled it, together split between the forces of Kongo who were both Dantor's antagonists, and Petwo... my partisans. Fierce the battle raged, a battle for freedom, and another unseen battle, a struggle for control! Side-by-side, Dantor was said to fight with the men, fighting with one hand only... for in the other she held tight her son-daughter.

Covetous of Dantor's power and skill, and jealous of her alliances, Mapyan betrayed her. With glee, Mapyan saw to it that Dantor's tongue was cut out so up until now she does not speak. Not satisfied by this treachery, Mapyan cut into her face... three marks she will forever carry. Blood ran into Dantor's eyes as she slipped into madness. Enraged, she broke free and seized upon Mapyan... stabbing at her again and again, stabbing her seven times over. But do not confuse her with Je Wouj (Red Eyed). This is none other than Erzulie Mapyan herself. Do not be deceived by the Liar." [40]

Dantor is said to have many lovers. One is her brother/twin named Jan Dantor (not to be confused with Ti-Jean Petro). Her child is sometimes called Ti-Jan Petro, the wild man of the Petro nation. His possessions are spectacular. At my kanzo, Ti-Jan took the head of a houngan and then leaped into the blazing Ogoun bonfire, snatched up a burning brand and proceeded to light the hair of the houngan on fire. I stood awe struck as the chwal ran around the poto mitan, his hair blazing. Ti-Jan then grabbed a

---

[40] Foucard, M. (2004) *La Legende de Loa.* Port-au-Prince.

gallon of clarin and using the brand as a source, blew fiery streams of liquid above the heads of the crowd. Having satisfied his fiery needs, Ti-Jan departed, leaving the exhausted houngan seated on the pé, his head smoking and glinting with embers!

Dantor's greatest love is said to be her youngest child, forever carried in her arms. This hermaphroditic child is so beautiful and wild, that s/he is considered to be fierce and inhuman. Feral would be a good word to describe him/her. She is said to be the messenger of Dantor's true will. Scholars and anthropologists have reported to the general public that the child is called Anäis. An interesting coincidence, as that is the same perfume that is a favorite of her mother's rival!

Erzulie Dantor's number is 7. In our house, we serve her with dark blue and gold, as well as the multi-colors of a patchwork dress; the manifestation known as Mambo Zila is known to wear red and green. And throughout Haiti, she is often served with denim blue and deep red -- the same as the flag of Haiti. Dantor's day is Tuesday, and she is feasted on several dates annually including July 16th (Saut d'Eau or more popularly, Sodo up in the Artibonite mountains), August 15th (Feast of the Assumption), and December 24th (Christmas Eve)

Her Catholic saint associations are with the Black Madonnas. As such, she also shares in their occult mysteries. The specific images used for Dantor are Our Lady of Czestochowa, Our Lady of Lourdes, Our Lady of Perpetual Help, and Our Lady of Mount Carmel. With the exception of Our Lady of Lourdes, Erzulie Dantor is most frequently associated with images of the Virgin Mary who carries an infant. Dantor is associated with Our

Lady of Prompt Succor, the patron deity of New Orleans. She is credited with turning away many hurricanes, sparing New Orleans.

Erzulie Dantor drinks kleren, trempe, dark creme de cacao, and black coffee. She is offered roasted peanuts and corn, rice and various beans, black beans and corn meal and kasava bread. Dantor receives the indigenous Kreyol female black pig. She carries a sharp silver dagger and smokes a pipe with tobacco, cigars or clove cigarettes. She receives as perfume Florida water or Rev D'Or. She enjoys all sorts of dolls, especially twin dolls being as she herself is a mother of twins (sometimes said to be Anaise and/or Ti-Jean).

Dantor is said to be single, though servitors align her with afore mentioned Ti-Jan Petro, Simbi Makaya and Ogoun Feray. She is a woman without man, a mother without father. She is both mother AND father, an allusion to her androgynous nature. She is the loving mother who nurtures and protects, as well as fights. Dantor is the one who rages and destroys, the mother who devours anyone who gets in her way. This is the side most feared, yet it takes a long time to reach this level of intensity. And when She does reach it, the level is very often justified.

Many priests claim she does fierce battle with her sister, Erzulie Freda Dahomey, and much has been written about their famous battles. But the simple fact is Freda is a city girl and Dantor is a country woman. Both like to play, but in different arenas. Dantor is a love 'em and leave 'em kind of woman, while Freda pines and flirts over her paramours. Dantor has no tolerance for such silliness and chooses partners who share her affinity for hard work and hard play. She is a power house Lwa, and one that we proudly serve here in the sosyete.

Simbi: Serpentine Magician

Simbi is the collective name given to a large group of spirits who hail from the Kongo region of West Africa. Scholarship is spotty for this amazing group of entities. There are arguments that state they are from the Taino cultures, descending from the zimis or spirits of the water ways in ancient Haiti. Other stories claim they are part of the Cymee legends in South Florida. Those legends speak of red hair, dark skins beings, child-like, who swim in the brackish waters of the everglades and take people away to teach them things.

Whatever his origin, Simbi is a spirit of fresh springs, streams, and wells. The name 'simbi' is the surname for a very diverse clan that includes Simbi Dlo, Simbi Andezo, Simbi Anpaka, Simbi Anpola, Simbi Lawouze, Simbi Maza, and Simbi Makaya. The relationship to fresh water for some of these is more or less apparent, and some, like Simbi Andezo (from the French *en deux eau* "in two waters") have a connection to both fresh and salt water. Others have no apparent connection with water at all.

Simbi Anpaka is associated with leaves and poisons. Simbi Makaya is known as a sorcerer, and when he enters the peristyle, the braided field whip is tied around him. Neither one are offered water. Some of the Lwa called Simbi may be served on the Rada point in some circumstances, though most are served in the Petro rites. While there are no female Simbi, the Lwa called Gran-n Simba is considered by some adepts to be the mother of all mysteries called Simbi. She is specifically tied to water. Her legends in Saint Marc speak of her being a water deity and daughter of Danbala[41.]

As a Kongo Lwa, Simbi brings his ancestral knowledge from the KiKongo area of West Central Africa. Kongo spirituality is a particularly sophisticated and creative outlook on the world. The Kongo religion divides the universe into two pieces. Heaven is thought to be the place of the gods and the earth the domain of the mortals. Between these two worlds lies a vast sea, an ocean of fluid that the Kongo spirits traverse in their movements between the two domains.

Kongo spirituality recognizes a unique spiritual hierarchy. Immediately above living humans are the ancestors, or Nkuyu. These are the ancestors who are named. Above them, and more removed from humans, are the Simbi. In the Kongo belief system, all Simbi (also called Basimbi for plural and Kisimbi) are associated with water. They are the source of special blessings but are known to be somewhat unpredictable. They are also said to be "twice born" which means that they have not lived recently on earth.[42] Hence, they are a higher class of ancestors, having been elevated by death to a higher status than humans, yet still available to us for consultation and service.

Wyatt MacGaffey, a leading scholar on Kongo culture, talks of how simbi spirits liked to perch in trees like birds and descend to the ground to create magic. It is not a big leap to envision the snakes of Haiti, perched up

---

[41] Foucard, M. J. (1981). *The Haitian Marroons: Liberty or Death*. Brooklyn, NY:Blyden.
[42] *www.inquincesweb.com*, accessed 4/5/04

in trees and descending to the ground when disturbed. Or Danbala, the great serpent, descending the poto mitan in the peristyle.

Michael Ortiz Hill, an American who was initiated as a Bantu tribal healer and writer postulates that "one of the more obscure words in American English is simbi, used only in the Georgia Sea Islands and the nearby coastal areas. Simbi has the same meaning in English as it has in Haitian Creole, in Cuban Spanish, in Brazilian Portuguese and in KiKongo. Simbi means "water spirit."[43]

And indeed, there is considerable scholarship about the "cymbees" of the southern wetlands, water spirits both fierce and magical, who inhabit streams, swamps and ponds[44].

The Vodou culture site lists no less than 27 names for Simbi, covering the nations of Rada, Petro and Kongo. The original simbis were cool, creative spirits in the Kongo cosmology. The magical ability of their pwen, called nkisi in Kongolese, translated into powerful magical practices. This magic moved across the oceans with the Africans and into Haiti, to merge with various groups in the Petro rites. We can find traces of it in songs for Simbi Anpaka, Simbi Gangan and Simbi Makaya.

Simbi Jèn Gangan, a nye!
Yo pe konn le Djab la ap monte Pwen an!

Simbi Jèn Gangan, deny it!
They are afraid the Djab knows my point!

---

[43] *www.gatherin.com*, accessed 4/5/04

[44] *www.mamiwata.com/waterspirits*, accessed 4/5/04

This song is a dare to Simbi Gangan, to deny that people know the power of the singer's pwen or point. And again:

Nèg Simbi Gangan, Nèg Simbi Gran Djab-la!

Men jenn Gangan vini sondè Pwen mwen!

Nèg Simbi Gangan, Nèg Simbi great devil there!

The young priest comes to test my point!

This song states that a young Vodou priest (the gangan) has arrived to test (sondè)the power of the singer's point. In both cases, the more powerful priest, Simbi Gangan has the ability to prove His worth via the pwen or point of the singer.

Every Simbi also has specific associations. Simbi Andezo has a connection to both fresh and salt water. Simbi Anpaka is associated with leaves and poisons. In our house, Simbi Makaya is known as a sorcerer, and is the patron of the Sanpwel Society. Although I have not come across any writing pointing to a female Simbi, I have a very close relationship with Gran Simba, who says she is the mother of all the simbis. As Simbi Makaya gave me her song and langaj invocation, I can hardly argue the point!

Elizabeth MacAlister wrote about her encounter with Simbi Gangan, in the mountains, high above Petionville, Haiti in 1993. Here is the song she reported the hounsi singing for him:

Simbi O Simbi Ganga E, m'a rele Simbi Ganga E
Yo mete pote kouto, yo mete pote poinya m'pap pe yo
Simibi Ganga e m'pap pe yo, Simbi Ganga!

Simbi O Simbi Ganga E, I'm calling Simbi Ganga hey!
They can bring knives, bring swords, I am not afraid of them,
Simbi Ganga I'm not afraid of them, Simbi Ganga!

In times of deep trouble, Simbi is the mercurial magician one can call upon to help facilitate closure to a problem at hand. Milo Rigaud writes brilliantly about this particular facet of Simbi's powers in Secrets of Voodoo:

"He is the voodoo Mercury who conducts the soul from the visible to the invisibles, starting from the crossroads, and who then leads the invisibles to the crossroads, to receive the sacrifice. The voodoo Mercury has the name of Simbi, a loa of many forms. He is the conductor of souls, who leads the souls of the dead in all directions bordered by the four magical orients of the cross. He is the Messiah of Legba, the messenger of the sun. Simbi corresponds to the hermetic Mercury of the cabalistic alchemy of the ritual sacrifice...Simbi is the creative principle of the seminal vesicle because, in Voodoo tradition, Legba as the center post is himself the principle of the magic wand." [45]

Simbi is known to be shy, standing outside the peristyle until coaxed in by the congregation. Some like Makaya are quite bellicose, talkative and gregarious. But in general, Simbi is shy like the snakes he is named for. Songs for Simbi speak of him being "hard to know."

Simbi Andezo! Sa ki fa yo pa vle we mwen, yo poko konnen, mwen

Yo bay mwen pwen a, Se pou m mache la nwuit O!

---

[45] Rigaud., *Secrets of Vodou*, p. 94

Simbi Andezo! They don't want to see me, they don't know me

They gave me the point, It is so I can walk at night O!

Simbi is also a Lwa of communication. He is associated with crossroads, thresholds and in between places. His vèvè encompasses an equal-armed cross, along with military style flags and stars, an allusion to his prowess as a strategist. There are many Simbi, so the colors favored for each Lwa will vary. In my peristyle, I was taught by Papa Fritzner to associate Simbi Andezo with turquoise and red; Simbi Makaya with red and black; Simbi Dlo with blue and green. I have also seen images of Moses used to symbolize Simbi. The explanation relates to the story of Moses casting his rod before Pharaoh and the rod turning into a serpent. Sosyete du Marche associates the Simbi nation with the image of the Three Kings. Simbi as a great magician syncretizes with the three mages for their perceived magical powers. Other houses use either Saint Barthol or Saint Gregory. Sosyete du Marche uses the image of Saint Charles Boromeo for Simbi Makaya (for the red and black robes the saint wears.)

Unlike Danbala Wedo who is imaged as a great serpent, large and resplendent in a tree top, the Lwa Simbi is anthropormorphisized as a long, slim ground snake. Whatever his image, Simbi is above all the preeminent magician, statesman and wise soul who brings power, wealth and insight to his servitors, as all serpent archetypes do.

Simbi's day of the week is Tuesday. He is served in Soukri (the stronghold of Kongo tradition in Haiti) on August 14th where the members go to bathe in a stream He is known to frequent. May 21st is his general fet in the countryside. The Simbis properly receive the native rooster and hen of Haiti grilled, white wine, soda and white candles. Andezo receives kleren, and red candles. You can also offer him water (if it is Andezo, offer water from two sources, such as ocean and fresh water), rain water, especially rain water from a lightning storm and snake skins.

Gran Bwa: The Island Beneath the Sea

All initiates of Vodou have a very special relationship with the Lwa Gran Bwa. He is the only Lwa with a face that is recorded through the auspices of his vèvè. That image is often one of a walking tree, with leaves for hands and a face above the large trunk.

Gran Bwa lives in the deep forest where the vegetation is wild. An old and venerable Spirit, he avoids contact with human beings. He is the protector of wildlife, and doesn't like to be seen. When called in a ceremony, Gran Bwa is generally not hungry, although the people prepare food for his pleasure. I think this offering of food to this Lwa is one of propitiation, to demonstrate the blessing he has conferred on a sosyete, to keep Him happy and to bestow honor to Him.

Envisioned as an anthropomorphic creature, he often takes a very long time to manifest in the peristyle during services. He is syncretized with Saint Sebastian in Catholic hagiography, for the tree Sebastian is pinned against. Gran Bwa is also the spirit of the Mapou tree which is the sacred tree in Vodou that connects the world of the living with the world of the ancestors and the Lwa. The center pole in a Vodou temple represents the holy Mapou tree. It is the highway the Lwa travel down, to visit the world of the living.

Gran Bwa'ss name is Creole for "Great Tree", implying Master of the Forest according to some authorities. This Lwa is one of the "Magical Three" Lwa who preside over the Kanzo cycle. He is also seen as a magician who has the curative powers of healing. Thus he holds a dual role in Vodou, because he knows the secrets of herbal medicine that the forest can offer, as well as the secrets of magic that the dark branches can camouflage.

The sacredness of certain trees in Haiti is one of the things that links the old African religions with the younger Northern European religions. Trees are not venerated as living Lwa, but as repositories of their ashe or power. Each Lwa has a specific tree which is dedicated to them. And it is Gran Bwa who rules over all these repositories, ensuring their safety, sanctity and continued growth for the Lwa and their servitors.

The mapou, or silk-cotton, tree is specifically sacred to Gran Bwa. It is not native to Haiti and was nearly decimated during the 1940 Anti-superstition Campaign, when many sacred trees were chopped down. The mapou survived and today is seen as the living embodiment of the African spirits. The mapou tree is envisioned as connecting the material and spirit worlds that the Africans called Vilokan. For lakous lacking a mapou, the tree is represented in the courtyard of Vodou temples by a central pole called the poto mitan. Gran Bwa is the guardian and protector of Vilocan, shielding the ancestors who have returned to rest beneath His metaphysical branches there.

Gran Bwa's altar very often consists of a cloth tied around a particular tree, at whose base offerings are left. As in pre-Christian Europe, trees are closely associated with the ancestors. They serve as a gateway to the residents of the Otherworld who have not yet returned to the living world, or who have chosen to remain in the Otherworld to act as guides and guardians of the living. This connection with the ancestors is what has given Gran Bwa ruler ship over the Ile (island) beneath the sea.

On that island resides the mighty Dead, awaiting rebirth into their new lives. It is an interesting exercise to think of the roots of the trees as branches in a world beneath our feet. But that is exactly how we perceive of Gran Bwa in Vodou. He is not so much a tree as He is a designation of place and time.

Gran Bwa's rites fall under the Petro style of service. He presides over the rite of Pile Fey ("Grind Leaves"), which is a part of the Kanzo cycle as well as the harvest. In our house, we serve Gran Bwa in the summer, when we harvest all the herbs in the lakou's yard. We have a large mortar and pestle dedicated to Gran Bwa that we use to grind down the many bundles into fine powders. It was cut from an large oak tree with proper ritual and carved for the sole purpose of Pile Fey. With its tall earthy appearance, thick bark covering and large striated bowl, it is the perfect vessel to convey Gran Bwa's ashe as we work and sing for the Lwa.

Pile Fey is also one of the many rites performed during Kanzo, hence the relationship of Gran Bwa to the kanzo cycle. Many, many leaves are needed – for the bathes of dissolution, for the offerings to the various Lwa, for the pakets tied during kanzo and for the food that is served to both men and spirits.

Gran Bwa is also a Lwa of healing. He is the power behind all the medicinal plants and forests of the world. This healing power is one of the mysteries of Kanzo, where he is addressed as Mèt Gran Bwa Ilé, the Lwa who ordains and prepares the hunyos for their participation in the kanzo cycle of the sosyete. His ceremony, which is not really a ceremony but rather the time of culmination in the spiritual journey of a candidate to priesthood, is held secret by all Kanzo candidates. Gran Bwa is solemn, austere and dignified. He asks questions, the answers of which determine whether the candidate is qualified to become a guardian of the ancestral tradition. He also establishes whether a candidate will or will not be given the secret of the asson and the gift of the eyes, called "priz de je."

There is an interesting correlation between the Haitian Gran Bwa and the African Dogon's Grand Bois. In the Dogon society of Mali, the entity called Grand Masque is also called Grand Bois and like in Haiti, he symbolizes the first mythical ancestor. In the prayers addressed to Grand Bois by the Dogons, they say that his words are the words of Mouno, their highest deity, who can be aligned with Bon Dieu. In Haiti, there is a song that goes:

Gran Bwa, sé gran moun yo , Gran Bwa sé gwo pawol.

Gran Bwa, it is a big man, Gran Bwa, there are big words

Serving Gran Bwa should properly be done in the woods, preferably at the foot of a large and venerable tree. He loves freshly cut leaves, branches and plants, particularly healing plants as offerings. Because herbs are raised as domestic crops, these belong to Azaka. But the wild plants of the world that heal such as vines, mushrooms and trees are the correct offerings for Gran Bwa. He will accept a very good cigar and drinks Kleren through his ear when he takes possession of his horse in service. Gran Bwa's colors are brown and green for the forests of the world, and his day for offerings is Saturday. He is syncretized with Saint Sebastian in the catholic hagiography, for the tree Sebastian is tied against.

These are the main Petro Lwa that we serve in our house. There are hundreds of others. The Petro nation is a large and ever evolving group. As we work with the island born spirits, we find there is always a new face coming forth asking for service. This is not a surprise to me. If we remember all the people who died to create the nation we know today, it begins to make sense that new spirits would arise from the Kalunga, to be served and fetted. Each of those spirits is someone who gave up their life to make Haiti what it is today -- a sovereign nation. As these indigenous spirits come forward (and I use that word to reflect any spirit that is tied to the land of Haiti), they require service for remembrance, healing and offerings. They need the blessing, the consecration of the services to help them on their own spiritual journey back to the Godhead. And they ask for remembrance of who they were, what they did and how they died. It is not much to ask of those who remain here. We would not have what we do, had these men and women not given their lives for it.

In the Petro style of service, we can serve all these brave men and women who fought so valiantly to set the nation of Haiti free. We serve by including them in our own worship. Vodou does not exclude them from remembrance. And neither do we.

Chapter Eight: The Guédé Nachon

Let me begin talking about the Guédé nation, by defining what a Lwa is or is not. That is because the largest confusion surrounding the Guédé group relates to their status as spirits. Let me also warn you that this nation's status is the most confusing aspect of Vodou. Many people simply throw up their hands and walk away at this point! I will be using a capital "G" when I refer to the Guédé as a group.

Let me set some terms out, to help illuminate the Guédé. A Lwa is an entity that was never alive. Danbala, Marassa, Legba are all Spirits who have never been corporeal, meaning they have no living counterpart that we know of. These entities are finite in number, and are an expression of larger truths in the world: Desire, Anger, Level Headedness. Their lives, the stories of their relationships and escapades, even their offerings and their colors are all symbols, signs and examples to help explain the larger truths that they express. A good comparison would be the Neters of Egypt – who are not just gods, but are expressions of reality, couched in story and legend. We could use the same expression for the Lwa of Vodou.

There are other entities that are erroneously referred to as Lwa. These are spirits who at one time were living people. A good example would be Don Petro, Makandal, Manbo Maynette. These spirits are archetypal reminders of the people they once were.

Don Petro is thought to have been a Portuguese slave owner or a slave himself. He lent his name (Pedor) to the rites he is believed to have created. Makandal is believed to have been the leader of the Rebellion that freed Haiti from bondage. Maynette is said to be the mambo who sacrificed the pig at Bwa Kayiman, starting off the revolution. These three individuals have been systematically removed from their historical context and fetted as one would the main Lwa of the Vodou pantheon. The results of serving them is often as startling as they are unpredictable. Mayanette comes into service screaming with bent hands, Makandal is silent, but leery of everyone. Don Petro moves with rapid steps, dancing ferociously around the poto mitan.

When the Haitian Ancestors encountered this type of spirit or force, they had no name for it because they knew it was not a Lwa. They might have said, "These things are mysterious. They are a mystery." From this identification came the process of naming the spirit as something different, using the moniker "mysteries" (or "miste" in Haitian Creole).

So we have two sets of spirits thus far -- Lwa (never alive) and "Mysteries" -- at one time alive, now dead. This category called "mysteries" also includes those spirits of the dead who are capable of working for a person, particularly a bokor. A spirit that works in this manner is elevated beyond the simple category of *Mort* (meaning dead). This spirit is called a *pwen achté* or a bought point. A bought point is a *misté* that has been captured and placed into a relationship with the purchaser. The buyer is often looking to gain something from the relationship with a pwen achte such as luck, power, love. But the relationship between the pwen and the buyer is a commercial one, and like any business deal, it can go sour as often as it can go well.

Zanset-yo (The Ancestors) can conceivably fall into either of these last two categories – "*mysteries*" or "*pwen achte*". What distinguishes ancestors is that they are your biologically related dead. They are your direct blood relations. They can and do work for you as your personal *misté*, but they can also work for others as *pwen achté*. For example, say your mom has passed away and is doing work for you. Your success with your mom's help encourages a family member to also appeal to your mom for help. The family member would either pay you to do the service for your mom, or give you some money to say thank you for letting your mom do the work for them. Either way, the exchange of money makes this a family *pwen achté* arrangement.

This *pwen achté* arrangement can also go the other way. A person not related to the family might see your success with Mom and try to buy her from a Bokor. This would not be possible if you keep up your end of the family service work. Meaning, you make an annual trek to her gravesite, maintain your non-corporeal relationship with her, and generally keep her happy, close and well loved. But not everyone does this, and so beloved family members drift off and become the source of pwen achte for unscrupulous priests who deal in such things. I assure you dear reader, as a priest of Ginen, my vows prevent me from ever doing this to anyone's family, especially my own! And we train each servitor in Sosyete du Marche to maintain their family allegiance, so just such a thing does not occur!

This difference between *pwen achté, misté,* Lwa and Guédé is at the heart of confusion in the categories of the dead in Vodou. In addition to the four groups just named, there are spirits who are elevated (meaning they have become Lwa) and are able to work for a person. These include your Met Tet, your Escorts and your personal constellation.

But it doesn't end there. Along with the afore mentioned categories, there are also the spiritual ancestors of a family line, all of whom gladly work for the person they are related to by blood. This would include not only relatives in recent memory, but relatives such as thrice great uncles and aunts, 4th cousins, twice removed, going back over generations. I like to think of this group as the Ethnic Ancestors. People we don't know intimately, but who by birth or by country are a part of your spiritual constellation.

And finally, there are those dead who are not elevated but are made to work. I call these the "mo'." This last group is treated separately from all the others. The structure of services, offerings and petitions for all these various components is complex and blurs the boundaries between all the various groups. This confusion is at the heart of the Guédé group.

Ethnic ancestors are served either with the biological ancestors or with the Lwa. Biological ancestors are served separately unless they are Elevated ancestors. Elevated refers to those ancestral dead who have had the full set of death rites, such as the Haitian Retire Mo Nan Dlo or the European Extreme Unction. Elevated also refers to those dead who are most likely to do work and those who rest with the Lwa in the Rada shrine of a given sosyete. The easiest way to understand this menagerie of dead, is to remember that those who have been venerated (meaning those who have had the full death rites) will be the most helpful. Or to put it simply, those dead who have been consecrated are served.

Confused? Good. Because no one should be working with the Guédé clan unless you are a kanzo mambo or houngan. This clan relishes their convoluted status and will gladly obfuscate the work of anyone approaching them who is not consecrated through Kanzo to this work!

So let me place them in the Priye so we know where they are served. The Guédé Lwa are technically served following the Rada Lwa. Remember, the Priye is a magical incantation that takes us all the way back to Ginen, to ancestral Africa. We saw how the Rada Lwa descended to earth (Legba, Marassa, Loko and Ayizan) and came across the waters to this world (Silibo Nouvavou, Agwe Tawayo and LaSiren). Upon their arrival, they left many dead behind them. Those dead are the Guédé and they must be acknowledged before they will allow us to continue to the Petro or island derived segment, which is the where the Africans landed in the new world.

But the Guédé are held distinct and separate for many of the previously stated reasons. Mainly, we keep them separate because they are not elevated; they have not had the cleansing rites of death that move them to a specific place in the hierarchy. Remember that many people died without their families knowing where their bodies were or without being able to properly bury them. Between the bodies of the dead from the Revolution and subsequent war engagements, there are many, many "unclaimed" dead in Haiti. The very ground beneath your feet encloses over 200 years of death and dying. You walk upon the shoulders of the dead each day in Haiti.

This distinction between the Guédé and other spirits makes certain Lwa uneasy in service, while others are downright disgusted. Most of the Rada Lwa will leave if a Guédé invades their party. Erzulie Freda will pointedly tell you this, if a Guédé happens to drop in on her party. Some of the stories say that Guédé is Azaka's more urbane but vulgar brother. Erzulie pretends to be rich and special. Guédé loves to reveal lies and untruths, and will happily speak his mind to anyone in earshot. Therefore, His favorite target is Freda with her fake French accent and her phony manners. Between Freda's sobs, Guédé's glee and the ensuing mayhem, Guédé can be a real downer at a Freda party!

Guédé altars are housed separate from the other Lwa. Again, the Guédés are not Lwa in the defined sense. They are the collective "unknown dead". Having no father or mother, having not received the final rites of death, they are the unclaimed freight of the spirit world. You do not place these characters with your beloved ancestral dead. It is a problem of semantics as we often do not distinguish the Lwa from "spirits" (who may be the spirits of the elevated dead). But, when there are ancestors involved, it is better to keep the 'family' together (meaning your direct ancestors who have received their death rites) and the wayward Guédé (who have not) apart on altars. I am not sure why exactly, though I would venture a guess to say that one doesn't feed strange spirits and family spirits together.

Papa Guédé is the titular leader of the pack. He lends his name to the entire group of spirits who share the surname 'Guédé,' and who are unique in that they are all considered to be the Spirits of death, resurrection and sexuality.

They relish the use of sexually explicit or otherwise socially inappropriate language and behavior. They don't care because after all, they are dead! What can we do to them? They are tricksters and love to clown around, making jokes and rude noises to get a laugh out of the crowd. But they also carry a slightly sinister air about themselves. I think it is because no matter how outrageous they are or how much fun they bring to the party, they are still death personified. And they remind us that we'll all end up just like them – dead after all.

The origins of the major Lwa in this family are obscure. There is current scholarship showing that the Guédévi people were the original inhabitants of the Abomey plateau. The Guédévi were Yoruba in origin. The closest in ethnicity today are the Mahis, but the culture of Guédévi did not survive in Africa. Historical texts have revealed that once they were conquered and in order to break their authority, the Guédévi were made to bury the dead, placing them at the bottom of the society. This can explain why up to this day they are known as guardians of the tomb. True to Fon religious ideals, the Guédé ancestors were incorporated into their theology as the "lords of the earth", and thereby lords of the dead who are buried within the earth. Later they were sold off as slaves because the Fon feared their magical powers.[46]

As many of the Guédévi were taken to Haiti as slaves during the Middle Passage, it is not hard to see how Guédé attained his position in Haitian Vodou[47].

A common conclusion historians have arrived at is that the Guédévis weren't big in numbers to begin with and were all sold into slavery by the Fons. Remnants of the Guédévis culture has been found in parts of Brazil, as well as Haiti. Bastide says that if their society remained in Africa after the Middle Passage, then they were absorbed completely by another group.

The Guédé as they became called in Haiti, are closely associated with The Baron, whose avatars are Baron Samedi, Baron

---

[46] Paul, Emmanuel C. (1962) *Panorama du folklore haitien.* Port-au-Prince: Imprimerie de l'Etat.
[47] Bastide, R. (1970). *African Civilisations in the New World.* London: C.Hurst & Co.

La Croix and Baron Cimetière. Depending on the tradition followed, The Baron is one of the Guédé; their spiritual protector who has raised them from the dead with the help of Baron Samedi's woman, Maman Brijit; or an aspect of the Guédé. In any of these configurations, Baron, Maman Brijit, and the Guédé rule death, the cemetery and the inhabitants of the cemetery.

In Haitian Vodou, the Guédé (also spelled Gédé or Ghédé) embody the powers of death and fertility. The family includes The Baron (who's avatars include the afore mentioned Samedi, LaCroix and Cimetière); Maman Brijit, the Baron's wife; and various Guédé such popular ones as Guédé Masaka, Guédé Nibo, Guédé Plumaj, Guédé Ti Malis, and Guédé Zaranye. Their preferred drum rhythm and dance is called the "banda". All of the spirits of this family, will enter the temple dressed funeral style clothing. Black threadbare clothing accented with purple or white and a pair of sunglasses is the preferred uniform. They love hats and powder their faces to give it the pallor of death. They might carry grave digging tools, sacks for begging and shrouds to roll around on. They like to use canes as phalluses, and they love to thrust their hips in the sexually explicit banda dance. They drink Piman, a concoction of raw rum or clairin to which twenty-one habanera or goat peppers have been added. In possession they will drink or rub themselves in the face, the eyes or even the genitals, proving that they are beyond mortal concerns.

The Guédé Nachon (nation) is said to have powers that reach beyond the grave, but all those powers are about death. It is a misconception that this nation of spirits has the ability to grant life. I have spoken with people who mistakenly serve the Guédé nation along with Danbala, thinking they are balancing the scales of life and death. Neither one has those abilities. And in fact, one negates the power of the other. Danbala's talent lies in creativity of the ancient, inspired kind. He allows you draw upon your innate talents through the wisdom of the ancestors. But in the presence of Guédé, those talents are diminished for Guédé brings catabolic energy to the table, which undoes the metabolic one of Danbala.

The Guédé Nation's real power lies in healing. They have the ability to change the course of illness and often will do so especially when children are involved. In a country like Haiti where there are often no doctors for miles around, the country people know they can call on Papa Guédé to help keep the ti-zanj (the little angels) safe from sickness and strife.

Unlike Papa Guédé, The Baron is unconcerned with healing or stopping death. He is Death itself and so he has no interest in the living other than when they pass through his hands to the other side. But the Baron holds an important place in the magical realms of the Vodou world. He controls the gates of Death. No Guédé may enter this realm without the Baron's express permission. Many times, The Baron must be called upon to come collect the unruly Guédé who show up at the end of the night to smoke and drink.

The Baron has a varied personality, according to whom you are talking. Some priests say that the Baron is too dangerous for anyone to speak with, that his realm of death is too cold, too eternal to call upon. One doesn't trespass with Death, least you bargain yourself away. I think it is a cultural bias, like so many things in Haiti. In a country where death walks with you daily, I would not trifle with the Baron either.

While Guédé is the gatekeeper of the cemetery, the Baron is death himself, and therefore the master of the cemetery, which Guédé guards. Deren called [Baron] the "eternal figure in black, standing at the eternal crossroads by which all men and even the sun must one-day pass." The Baron, and his wife Maman Brijit are the heads of the Guédé family. They are apparently not of African origin, but are Kreyol, and may in fact be related directly to the Taino Indian ancestors.

The Baron tends to be more serious, and in this, also more sinister than his children the Guédé. He is a powerful sorcerer, and a Bokor must ask his permission before capturing the soul of a person to create a zombie. The Baron is intimately tied, along with the Lwa Gran Bwa and Kafou, to the secret societies in Haiti[48].

The Baron has many aspects - Baron La Croix (Baron the Cross) is the mystical Baron responsible for the reclamation of souls. This Baron is the one who brings the dead safely across the Abysmal Waters to Ginen. Baron Samedi is involved in the magical ceremonies of the Sanpwel, including those in which the punishment of zombification is inflicted on criminals. Baron

[48] Davis, W. (1997). *The Serpent and the Rainbow.* Clearwater, FL:Touchstone

Kriminel works for pay, and must be paid by the end of the year, November 2, the Feast of the Dead. Baron Cimetière is another avatar who rules the cemetery proper, itself a crossroad of magic and power. Where the first three Barons have influence and power over the human body, Cimetière is more like an idea or concept, having control over the mystical road of the dead. One does not serve Cimetière so much as pay him for the ability to pass safely through the land of the dead. All the avatars of the Baron carry His imagery -- tall, austere, gaunt, dressed like a gothic funeral director in black. I was taught that unless you have The Baron in your constellation or were born on his day (November 2) then you do not serve Him. He is too dangerous to anyone He has not chosen for himself. Even those of us who do serve him, must pay the price in the end for that service.

The Baron is paired with an equally strong and powerful female counterpart known as Maman Brijit. Despite a popular myth travelling the web, Maman Brijit is not tied to the Irish saint of the same name. No one I am familiar with in Haiti can definitively tell me where Maman Brijit came from. I think much like her husband, she is a Kreyol Lwa, arising out of the pain and suffering of the Africans on the island of Haiti before the revolution.

Maman Brijit can be seen as an "allegorical personification of the moral force in the Haitian Vodou judicial system.[49]" Maman

---

[49]   *http://www.thesevenafricanpowers.com/Binah-Read.html*,   accessed 8/20/2011

Brijit is said to live in the cemetery, and she is known as the consummate judge of life's affairs -- moral, medical and monetary. Her devotees say she lives in a cairn of stones, beneath either the *Figye Maudit* (Autograph tree) or a *Bwa Dom* (West Indian Elm tree.) Onto either one, they tie strips of fabric in the branches, place stones wrapped in paper on which they've written petitions to her. They place these on her cairn and pray for justice for their sons and their families.

I find this point most interesting. A Lwa of judgment lives within the very crossroads of life and death. Within the walls of the cemetery lie all the knowledge, experience and power of the dead that can be called upon for healing, balance and justice. Maman Brijit can call upon any of these dead for their opinion, their help or to intercede in an affair. She carries within her grasp the very decision of life and death, making her a fitting partner for The Baron. Together, They rule with impunity the place where one day we will all reside.

I believe that Maman Brigitte is the epitome of non-conformist behavior in a female. She has to be tough and strong, she is married to Death. In possession, Brijit is raunchy and often slyly suggestive, but at the same time, she is powerful, commanding respect. She often must make life and death decisions. "Maman" translates to "Mother"; she is the Mother of all Guédé (ancestral) lwa and of the dead.

Brijit is also revered for her ability to bring about healing -- physical, mental and spiritual. Vodouisants approach her to request healing from life-threatening circumstances. She has the power to bring people back from the brink of death.

In Maman Brijit we see a strong woman who can be an inspiration for all of us, teaching us that it's OK to be both a mother, a wife as well as an independent person. Maman Brijit is not easy to pin down into stereotypes. She is a devoted mother and wife; a stern parent with a firm hand; a licentious drinker with a foul mouth; a red hot mama who is as casually flirtatious as she is bawdy.. Maman Brijit shows me that you don't have to lose your own identity in a relationship or in your duties. You can be a Mom, a lover, a doctor, an artist or all of the above. You can have multiple roles and still be you.

Maman Brijit often manifests in possession as a hard drinking, tough talking woman. She smokes clove cigarettes and drinks fiery Piman or any rum in which hot peppers have been soaking. Not one to mince words, she gives strong opinions when asked and is cold in her judgments. She is intolerant of people who cannot come to a decision, and makes very hard choices for folks when asked to do so. Approach her with caution, for she does not speak in sweet tones or nor does she candy coat it.

With The Baron and Maman Brijit using a strong guiding hand, it figures that their 'first born' son would be a handful. The story goes that there were so many dead in Haiti, the Baron had his hands full keeping them under control. He plucked one soul out of the teeming dead and called him Guédé Nibo. Papa Guédé, or Guédé Nibo (and also spelled Nivo) is supposedly the corpse of the first man who ever died. He is recognized as a short, dark man with a high hat on his head, a cigar in his mouth and an apple in his left hand. Papa Guédé is a psychopomp who waits at the crossroads to take souls into the afterlife. Some folks say these spirits are the dead from the Middle Passage to the New World. Others state they are the dead from the slave and revolutionary times. I think some of this is true, but the real dead that I feel Guédé Nibo gives voice to are the ones that are pertinent to you. And like the Baron, he has many permutations.

Guédé Masaka assists Guédé Nibo. He is an androgynous male or transgendered gravedigger, recognized by his black shirt, white jacket, and white headscarf. Guédé Masaka carries a bag containing poisonous leaves and an umbilical cord. He is sometimes depicted as the companion of Guédé Oussou.

Guédé Oussou wears a black or mauve jacket marked on the back with a white cross and a black or mauve headscarf. His name means "tipsy" due to his love of white rum. Guédé Oussou is sometimes linked with the female Guédé L'Oraille.

There are even reports I've seen of a female Guédé named Guédélia. She is a small, young girl, tough talking with a foul mouth and a street smart way about her. She reminds me of a young goth, only with much more attitude. I do not know anything more about her, or what kind of healing she offers.

Vodou theology states that children are "*petit lezanj*" (little angels) and are not meant to suffer. They are innocent. When Papa

Guede is called to treat a sick child, he does so with all seriousness. It is believed that he will not take a life before its time, and that he will protect children. Mama Lola's children were overshadowed by her Papa Guédé. He took a special interest in all they did. But Papa Guédé is also very crass, nosey and gossipy. He has a talent for mind reading, and knows everything about everyone, living or dead. And he doesn't hesitate to spill the beans about anything. This last talent makes him a less than perfect guest at parties.

Guédé Bábáco is supposedly Papa Guédé's lesser known brother. Like Guédé, Bábáco is also a psychopomp, ferrying the dead across the waters. He does not have the healing abilities of his brother. Instead, he works to help the dead cross over.

In Vodou theology, Guédé is considered to be the primal or "root" ancestor of us all, having been the first of the mighty dead reclaimed by The Baron from the waters of Ginen. As Mama Lola says, "Everybody got Guédé!"[50] Because of this, Guédé is privy to the knowledge and experience of all the ancestors who dwell in your (his) house (the cemetery). It is he who gives voice to the unnamed and forgotten dead of your lineage.

In possession, Guédé has a tendency to multiply. Because he gives voice to the unnamed and forgotten dead, there have appeared many Lwa with names such as Guédé Djanmensou (never

---

[50] Brown, K. (2001). *Mama Lola: A Vodou Priestess in Brooklyn*. Berkeley: University of California Press.

drunk), Guédé Kache Bo Lakwa ("hidden behind the cross"), Guédé Ti Pous Dlo (little flee in the water), Guédé Ti Malis (little mischief), and so on. When the Guédé manifest in the temple, they will proceed to dance lasciviously, sing and tell dirty stories or jokes. They love to call out someone and tell everyone present the most embarrassing fact of that poor person's life. They do not lie and they love to be gossips.

Serve the Guédé nation on Fridays, and on November 2, their particular feast day. Our house uses the image of St. Martin de Porres for the Baron. Maman Brijit does not have a specific image that is used to represent her. Our house uses an image of St. Brighid dressed in black with her crooked flail and downcast eyes. I know some houses also use St. Rita, becuase of the skull in the picture. And for Guédé Nibo, we use St. Gerard Majeur, for the black cassock and the cross in his hands.

Feed this group rice with black beans, salt mackerel, sweet potatoes, cassava bread and white pudding. Lots of strong black coffee and of course, their beloved Piman. If you do not have the Piman recipe, then place 21 habanera peppers in a bottle of kleren or white rum. Be sure not to drink it yourself -- this is a bottle for the Guédé only.

The Guédé are part of everyone's constellation. They are everywhere in the world. The Baron may manifest as the tough talking manager at the grocery store, ruling over all the high school checkout girls and boys. Papa Guédé will manifest as your tippling uncle who tells dirty jokes at your mother's brunch on Sunday.

Maman Brijit will appear as the cold stern boss who delivers pink slips without flinching. They are all here with us on this earth. We need only be aware to see them as they stroll through life along side of us. They assure us not to take life to seriously, to lighten up and be glad for what we have today. Their presence is a sign that life as we know it has many levels and layers. And they will always be there, to help us make the hard choices, to rejoice when we do and to point out our fragilities when we do not.

Chapter Nine: Concentric Circles of Power

In Vodou, we speak of concentric circles of power. These circles are present throughout the structure and organization of the religion. They are multi-dimensional, interconnected and reflect the world of Vodou very accurately. They can be placed upon the physical lakou itself. Upon the liturgy of the faith, even upon the style of service one encounters over the course of a liturgical year. These 'circles' all center on the poto mitan, the center post of the peristyle proper.

The faith of Vodou does not have physical representations of the spirits. Catholic iconography has been adopted over time, but in fact, the spirits themselves do not have a physical image on earth. This has led to the adoption of a symbol that represents the entry point for the spirits into the world of humanity. The poto mitan, with its uplifting imagery of a world tree, holding the ceiling of the temple in place, becomes the entry point where the Lwa descend into the peristyle. Often carved with serpentine designs meant to represent Danbala and Aida Wedo, it sits center to all the activity of the houmfort, or in some cases, the peristyle proper.

Poto mitans can be very elaborate or simple affairs. I have seen poto mitans made of cement and painted with nothing but a stripe. I have danced around elaborately carved ones with entwined snakes and vines dripping down. One temple uses a stack of old drums as theirs. Another has no physical poto, but draws a beautiful veve on the floor and surrounds it with offerings. Still another hangs a series of ribbons and vines to center their work around. The poto mitan can also be a simple tree trunk, cut and stood in the center of the temple. Sosyete du Marche's poto mitan is a brick pillar, supporting our house (literally). All poto mitans are simply imitations of the real one - the holy mapou tree is the physical poto mitan for many houmforts.

One kisses the poto mitan when entering the peristyle of a house. It is a sign of humility and reverence, for this is the virtual doorway to Ginen, where the Lwa descend to be with their servitors.

For purpose of our discussion, I've created a two dimensional peristyle. In the center we see the poto mitan, the center post around which everything moves and the energy of a ceremony is seated. Looking at the left side of the diagram, we see that the ring surrounding the poto mitan has the word "peristyle" in it. The next link outward in a temple space is the peristyle proper, the actual building that houses the poto mitan. In some locations, this building is enclosed on all four sides, giving the people inside privacy to work. In the Haitian countryside, a peristyle can be open on all four sides, allowing breezes to come in and freshen the air. In Haitian cities, peristyles often are below ground, to take advantage of the cooler temperatures. In all cases, the roof top of the space where the peristyle is located is called the tonnel and the poto mitan often reaches from the floor up to the tonnel.

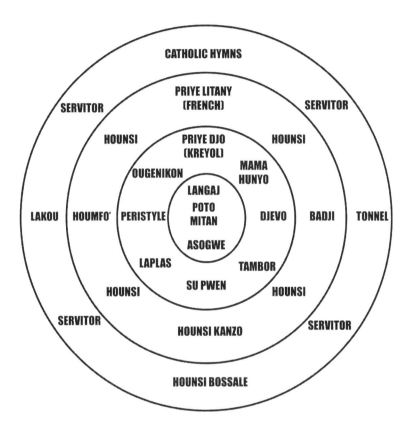

The third ring from the center contains the word "Houmfort". This refers to the physical collection of houses, kay Lwa (house of the Lwa) and out buildings that a sosyete may have on their property. In our case, the houmfort is our physical house with the temple located in our basement. And in the city, where peristyles are often tucked away in a subbasement or down a back alley, the houmfort is a metaphysical reference to the space that encloses the temple.

Finally, in the last ring, we see the word "Lakou," which means "yard." In the Haitian country side, that would be the physical ground that all the previous items sit on. In the city, it means the land the home is built on. At our houmfort, it refers to the acre of ground surrounding our house. The "yard" is the physical embodiment of Ginen in the new world. Its confines protect and seclude both the Lwa and the servitors. There are many songs about someone or something being in the yard that does not belong there. That is because the lakou is considered sacrosanct and as such, is said to be invincible to malefic work. When you are on the lakou of a temple, you are on sacred ground.

If we look from the outer ring to the inner, we see that the "Lakou" encloses the "Houmfort", which contains the "Peristyle" that shelters the "poto mitan." Like a set of nesting dolls, each circle encloses the next, containing the power and keeping it at the heart of the property.

Often, beneath the tonnel, there is a building dedicated to the spiritual work of the sosyete. This building is usually comprised of individual rooms that are dedicated to specific uses and purposes in the sosyete. There is a space set aside for the Rada spirits, as well as one for the Petro nations. These rooms are called "Badji," and they feature altars set up for the specific Lwa of each nation that the sosyete serves. There is also a space called the

"Djevo." This is the sacred birthing chamber of initiates, and no one may enter this space who is not kanzo. These spaces and their ranking can be seen in the ring to the right of the Poto mitan diagram. If we move from the Poto mitan to the next ring, we find the Djevo, the Inner Adytum (the holy sanctuary) of the peristyle. The djevo is often surrounded by Badjis, the sacred altar rooms of the Lwa. And finally, the all of the previous is enclosed by the covering protection of the tonnel.

Each ring defines the inner and outer aspects of the religion. Servitors start on the outside of the temple, as visitors and observers to services. They then move into the role of Hounsi, the first rank one can take as a kanzo of the faith. (Kanzo is covered later in this chapter.) Hounsi eventually becomes Su Pwen. And after a proper length of study and practice, Su Pwens become Asogwe, and can sit before the poto mitan to speak to the Lwa. So again, we see the concentric progress of ranks and rites within the religious framework of Vodou.

A final note is about the congregation itself. The servitors move into the next circle to become hounsi, then move again to the next circle to assume important roles within the sosyete. These roles include the Tambor who presides over the drums; the La Plas who is the master of the ceremonies, and is responsible for knowing the vèvès and how to draw them accurately; the Ougenikon who is the choir master and keeper of the sosyete's songs and the Mama Hunyo who cares for the kanzo candidates.

Each of these rings accurately reflects the relationships of the house to one another.

At the edge stand the observers who I named 'servitors' on the diagram. The saying is if "you're in, you're in. But if you're out, you're out." And this is a verbal reflection of the concept of circles within circles. The idea of concentric rings of power are also contained within the servitor themselves.

Your personal set of concentric circles begins with the Ancestors at the center. The ring of the Met Tet does enhance your Ancestral spirits. I said earlier that the Met Tet is you in heaven. It is also a reflection of your own ancestral lineage. A child of Freda might have a strong matrilineal line. Ogoun kids have service or even military members in their background. Earth reflects the heavens. We are the sum of all our parts and the Met Tet holds the key to understanding it all. Within your blood, your own DNA, stand your blood Ancestors. This is as close as it gets for a bond to exist between you and the Spirits. Surrounding the Ancestors is the Met Tet with all its power, escorts and influence. This ring enhances, modifies and influences the inner one.

Outside of the Met Tet's sphere, would be the escort ring, that group of Spirits who choose to walk with you in this life and beyond. And finally, surrounding all of it, are the rasin Lwa, those spirits that are inherited through your family root line. Your own personal set of concentric circles perfectly reflect the same construct as the peristyle or the liturgy. In looking at these notes, we create our own concentric circle around ourselves, with both our spirits, our liturgy, our community and finally, our own family.

But the concentric circle paradigm rules not only the physical building or the participants. It also orders the manner in which a service is run. The seating arrangement in a peristyle is hierarchal in nature. The Asogwe rank sits closest to the Poto mitan, allowing those whose heads have been properly consecrated to be the closest to the power source. Behind them sit the SuPwens, the next level of consecration behind the Asogwe. Behind them are the hounsi, who are the lowest level of consecration and who are the majority of heads in a given sosyete. And finally, guests and bossales sit to the rear, their heads unmarked for the Lwa, their power minimum at best. This arrangement was the rule when we were in Haiti and it is also a part of any given ceremony.

At a recent Fet Guédé, we sat in the place of honor as guests, but we were arranged so that the Houngan and I sat closest to the poto mitan and the hounsi sat down the row from us. The presiding mambo and her group of Asogwe snugged up tight to the altar, to protect the vèvè they were consecrating and to allow just their house asogwe the room to do their work uninhibited. When the time came to do the public prayers, the group broke up and I was invited to stand and salute with them. My rank allowed me to join them for the public portions, but for the private work, I was relegated to the position of spectator same as everyone else.

What I find particularly interesting is when the paradigm plays out without any effort on the part of the participants. At a service two years ago in Jacmel, the concentric circle formed over and over again all night, and I doubt anyone was deliberating trying. It just seemed to happen. As the evening tore into a fiery round of Petro drumming, the Lwa descended and took their horses with charming élan.

One elderly mambo in particular caught my eye. Her ancient face had smoothed out, the deep creases disappearing as the Lwa settled over her. She stood straight and danced with great ease and grace. She was very close to the poto mitan and kept touching the center post with her left hand, swirling around and around, like a ballerina dancer in a jewelry box. Just outside the reach of her right hand, the Houngan kept a steady rattling with his asson, enticing the Lwa to keep moving, dancing and shedding its ashe for the group. Behind him danced a group of three hounsi, who held their mesmerized eyes on the Lwa as she twirled effortlessly around the poto mitan. And behind the hounsi, were the drummers, who maintained a steady beat, allowing the Lwa her time and grace to bless us all with her presence. Four concentric circles assembled without effort or even consciously trying. The Lwa eventually exited, and the mambo returned to her former self, smiling shyly and sitting down from her exertions. The drummers broke for a cigarette and the hounsi drifted off to flirt with the young men at the edge of the tonnel. When the drums picked up again, another group formed and so it went for the night. Each time, a series of four circles formed, with the Lwa at the center and the power drifting outwards toward the assembled visitors.

The paradigm of concentric circles is most evident in the rank and structure of the membership of a peristyle. There is a Senior elder who is always an Asogwe priest. Their Met Tet quite often is the patron of the houmfort. Although traditional houses in Haiti often serve several Lwa who are pertinent to their lineage, in our sosyete, the Patron made Himself known many years ago and became the guiding principle for us. As such, we have kept His energy as the mainstay of the house. But there can be other Lwa who are honored as well.

Returning to the concentric circle diagram on page 217, we see that the next circle out contains the asogwe priests. Asogwe has learned to take care of themselves, the spirits and others, through public service, monthly ceremonies, and community outreach. They are outwardly focused, having worked to achieve their rank through selfless service to others.

The next circle contains the su pwen priests. This rank takes care of themselves and the spirits. They are the hardest rank to hold, as they are always working with the asogwe for the community, the congregations and of course for themselves through ancestor services and Met Tet work.

The third outer circle contains the hounsi kanzos, who are learning to take care of themselves and their own ancestral spirits. Hounsis are the backbone of any sosyete, and deserve a huge share of the credit for the operation, functionality and cohesiveness of any Vodou sosyete.

Finally, there are the Sevis Tets. This particular rank is where we (Sosyete du Marche) place those folks who are not ready to commit to a kanzo, but wish for a deeper relationship with their own Met Tets and ancestors. We strive toward elevating balanced people with a focus on family and the future. To this end, we do not kanzo anyone under the age of twenty eight years. We have found over the years we have worked as priests, that people need those years to find their footing, finish school, get a job and become productive in their lives. By the time they reach twenty eight, they have lived life a little, travelled a little and generally gotten a feel for where they want to be in the world. Having achieved some personal goals first, we think, is the right time in which a candidate can begin to conceive of their work as a servitor of Vodou.

Each rank comes with rights, privileges and responsibilities that are established according to skills, knowledge and capabilities of the given candidate. And each rank sits within its own Circle of Power, in perfect alignment with all the rest.

Along with the ranking of members, the set up of the peristyle and the way ceremonies unfold, the very liturgy itself is also a set of concentric circles, spiraling the participants inward, ever closer to the poto mitan, ever tighter to the Divine mystery they wish to embrace. The Priye Ginen, the ancient prayer of Africa is also a clear demonstration of the concentric circle theme.

We begin in French, with Catholic hymns. These old, venerable songs are snatches of older tunes that are no longer used in modern liturgical rituals. Some are from the Enlightenment period, while others seem older. It would be an interesting research project to trace the origin of the hymns sung. Someone remarked that one point in all the discussions of Vodou that is often missed, is that the colonial plantation masters all came out of 17th and 18th century France. That time frame would provide an interesting insight into the liturgical make up of the Priye today, as well as provide a source for the inspiration of things such as the chromolithographs of the saints, ritual handshakes and other esoteric touches that style a Vodou ceremony.

The Catholic canticles then give way to what is called the Priye Djo or recitation of the Catholic saints. This listing of begins with male saints and then follows with female saints. It is edited at each house, according to the Lwa served and the saints honored.

The Priye Djo is followed by the Priye Ginen, the listing of all the Lwa who are served in a sosyete. This list includes what I call the major Lwa such as Legba, Marassa, Loko and Ayizan and then diverges into the various nations of spirits, including such luminaries as the Nago nation, home to Ogoun and the Kongo nation of Simbis. This listing continues until all the important spirits have been named.

The recitation then moves to the Dead, beginning with the Baron and the Guédés and finishing up by listing all the dead of the house in order of their demise.

There is a prelude segment that then leads into the Kreyol portion of the prayer, where the Lwa who rose from the island of Haiti are then named. They are revolutionaries such as Mambo Cecile Fatiman who was instrumental in the Battle of Verities. Makandal who was said to have begun the war with his guerilla tactics and poisons plants.. They are natives of the island like Ti-Jean and the ancient *caciques* or Caribbean Indians who were remembered by older houses on the island. We are going backwards in time, back to the era of pre-slavery, when the island of "Ayiti" was without invaders and ruthless land owners. The circle continues to spiral inward, as we finally come to the original words of the prayer and power.

We have arrived at the section known as *langaj*, where we begin to speak in the forgotten language of African tongues. As we move closer in ritual to the mythical land of Ginen, we speak the language of the Lwa themselves – the royal tongues of the courts of Africa, the words and phrases of the first enslaved Africans brought over by the Portuguese traders so long ago. When we sing this portion, we have arrived back in land of the Spirits themselves; in the place we call Ginen. This land never truly existed. It is the myth of a land that is pure and wholesome, a place where the Africans could escape to, if only in their minds. Here reside the Ancestors of myth and memory. Here live the Lwa in their palaces of word and song. And here is where we begin the real work of serving, so that the Lwa will come and be with us.

It is a remarkable feat that has been handed down to us today by these ancient men and women. The Africans had nothing and yet they managed to create a faith of such beauty and inspiration, it continues to live today as a stellar example of what can be achieved when people from diverse backgrounds put aside their differences and find commonalities to rally around. Their gift was to demonstrate that ordinary men and women can work together toward a common goal and not only achieve that goal, but reach beyond it, placing themselves among the hallowed company of the Divine messengers of God. By employing the gift of communion, they showed that men and women can become more than mere mortal bodies; they can walk among the immortals and for a brief moment see the potential good in all of us.

The Ancient Africans achieved this by creating a style of service that gave every nation its place, and allowing everyone present to find that place where they could speak to the Divine.

The organization of a Vodou ceremony is an ambassadorial affair. Like an audience before a king, each person or empire must be properly presented, their name and rank identified, and their presence propitiated accordingly. The Lwa are very much the ambassadors from Ginen. Each set of spirits represents the nation of Africans that brought Them to the New World. Studying the Lwa origins, stories, family histories and natures helps us to learn not only about them, but how to work and serve them properly.

This familiarity with the family of the Lwa also helps us to put them in correct theological placement in the Reglemen. The placement is remembered in the Priye Ginen, the blueprint for all Vodou services. The Priye lays out in very clear terms where all the various nations of Spirits are called.

Because the Priye is an oral teaching, it has not been written down until very recently. This lack of a written record I feel, was the stumbling block to understanding the differences in styles of service and how each nation is honored in a given ceremony. Although you can find long listings in older books, they often omitted the crucial pieces of evidence that pointed toward the inclusiveness of the rites. The authors had no idea what they were actually listening to, and simply wrote down brief versions, omitting various parts of the Priye Djo which lists all the actual nations served. Admittedly, the language was also a barrier. Between the opening French prayers, the kreyol litanies and the closing langaj verses, if the listener was not a linguist, then they'd have had no clue as to what they were hearing.

This verbal bricolage caused many anthropologists to simplify their findings and to lose track of the many nations that contributed to the rites. Most of the older academics like Metreaux or Courlander, gave us a very simplified view of a service. They divided the working into two sections - Rada and Petro. These divisions were further simplified into cool for the Rada and hot for Petro. As time went on, these descriptions evolved into tones such as sweet, nice and helpful for the Rada, with hot, angry and vengeful for the Petro. Although there are elements of "hot" and "cool" in both the Rada and Petro nations, this is a gross simplification of each one's style of service.

To begin to comprehend the sophisticated theology of a Vodou service, we must understand the makeup of the Africans who came to the new world via the slave trade. A little history will help make this distinction clear.

The name Rada is from the city state called Alarada in Dahomey, Africa. Although the Rada Lwa are a dominant group of spirits served in Haitian Vodou, the arrival of Dahomean Africans made up less than 25% of the slave populations during the plantation era.[51] The Rada nation or nachon as we say in kreyol, came from the northwest coast of Africa, south of the Sahara Desert. It included the nations of Adya, Awousa, Banbara, Bini, Ewe, Foula, Ibo, Mede, Nago, Oyo and Siniga. Each of these nachons had its own dialect, spirits and ceremonies. Today, these nations are known by their more modern names -- Cote d'Ivoire, Benin, Togo and Ghana.

Kongo refers to the area of West Africa south of the Kalahari Desert and includes people from Kongo, Angola, Bengal, Lowango, Mayonbe, Moundong and Pemba. Today, we know this area as Nambia and Botswana. Most nachons were comprised of a dominant ethnic group, foreign laborers and war captives. As a

---

[51] Manning, Patrick (1993). Migrations of africans to the americas: the impact on africans, africa and the new world. *The History Teacher*, 26(3), 279-296.

---

result, the West African coastline was a multilingual melting pot of nations, who all gave their spirits, words and practices to what we know today as Vodou. We see this in the presence of Arabic, Nago and Awousa words in the songs. Not only are these elements a testimony to the mixing of groups, but it shows that they lived side by side in Africa.[52]

Scholarship also shows that groups in Africa did not fight for land, but for laborers. The wars of the Kongo kings in particular, captured large numbers of neighboring laborers and held these people in prison pens for years. This was one of the many sources the Portuguese mined for slaves, when they landed at Bight of Benin.

This mixing of nations, peoples and languages, is the heart and soul of Vodou today. We know of these nameless men and women by their birth places. There are extant newspaper advertisements from the colonial period for runaway slaves that name not only tribal affiliations, but brands, markings and other symbols on the body to be used to identify the slave. These odd bits of adverts and knowledge help us today identify the many nations that came into the islands.[53]

---

[52] John Thornton, J. (1998). *Africa and Africans in the Making of the Atlantic World 1400-1800.* New York: Cambridge University Press.
[53] Fouchard, J.(1981). *The Haitian Marroons: Liberty of Death.* Brooklyn, NY:Blyden.

All these African nations gave rise to the sophisticated and elegant theology of Vodou today. Let us take a look at some of the ceremonies of Vodou, to see how these African remembrances play out in them.

Rada rites are said to be the cooler, more beneficent and magnanimous portion of service. They honor those Nations and Lwa who are African in origin and familial in nature. The Rada Lwa tend to be more balanced, often occurring in pairs, and descending from royal antecedents in Africa.

These royal pairs are reflected in the Rada rite through the mirrored gestures of the priests and the tolke or asson gestures. The double energies of the Rada nachons are seen in the duality of the Rada vèvès, which are drawn with great care to be exactly the same on both sides. Even the physical drawing of the Vèvè is mirrored in hand and gesture. The pairing is further seen in the handshakes and salutes given by priests to one another and the mirrored vres or twirls of the hounsis. All the ritual gestures, flourishes and moves in the Rada Rite are outer signs of the duality that is inherent through the Lwa themselves.

Rada rites are considered the cooler sections of the service. This is because a cool head is considered a powerful one, and the kings of Africa who ruled, had to be level headed in order to be powerful and just rulers. Rada rites are dominated by the yanvalou as the major drum rhythm, with some different interpretations used according to the songs being sung. The yanvalou drum beat is a smooth, rolling cadence, that gives rise to the same in songs and singing. The easiest pattern to recognize and learn, yanvalou anchors the beginning of the service with its steady 3-4-1 beat.

The Yanvalou is also the name of a dance that is performed for the Rada nation of spirits. Dancers bend over, as if bowing low before a king. Their backs undulate like a serpent, moving slowly and stately. A dozen or more white clad dancers, performing the yanvalou around the poto mitan of a temple, look very much like a great white serpent, encircling the peristyle. This dance represents the ritual gesture that is given to royalty. It is meant to be a representation of the Lwa Danbala, encircling the floor with His holy presence. The yanvalou dance and drum beat are both the anchor and the heart for the liturgical structure in this section of the service.

Rada services feature drums played with hands, on cow hide heads. In Haiti, our sosyete had two different sets of drums, with one dedicated to Rada and one to Petro services. The rada drum set was larger, with big bellied bodies and large heads. The cow hides were tied on with raffia rope and held down tight with large wooden pegs. I remember the drummers holding the drums over the fire before service, to help dry and tighten the heads onto the bodies of the drums. In a damp and humid area like the Jacmel coastline, keeping those drum heads tight was all night job. There was no metal on the Rada set at all. The heads were adjusted by pounding the pegs in at various times throughout the night. The drums are fuller sounding to my ears, and they were often accompanied by someone playing a cow bell with a stick.

Rada services are lead by the houngan or mambo playing an asson and bell. In Africa, bells were used by authority figures to gain attention in courts, marketplaces and at gatherings[54]. The Dahomean word for bell is gan, which is also the suffix on the title of the priest. The Asson is created from the kalbas kouran, literally "running gourd" an appropriate name for this leafy vine that grows abundantly throughout the island of Haiti. The fruit of the vine yields a rounded bulb with a short stubby handle. Dried and polished, the gourd is hollowed out and covered with a net of beads and snake vertebrae that are shaken to call forth the Lwa. The asson and its accompanying bell are the heart beat of a Rada ritual and all newly Kanzo mambos and houngans are taught the finer points of holding and using the asson properly.

White, the color of coolness, purity and royalty is used to represent a Rada service. The servitors gather in crisp white clothing, their heads tied with white satin mushoirs. The tables are laden with white foods. Rada services have the look of a High Tea to me. There are often many pastries, dainty finger size cakes, top shelf liquors and piles of fresh fruits and candies. Coffee is served with cream and sugar. All the offerings are set out on white china plates, with white linens and good silverware. Vases of fresh

---

[54] Vansina, J. (1969). Bells of kings. In *The Journal of Aftrican History.*10 (2), pp 187-197.

flowers always are present and brand new white candles are lit to honor all the Lwa. Sometimes, there are additional colors present as well. Freda with her pink and pale blue. Loko with yellow. Agwe and Siren with their sea blues and greens. That second color shifts from temple to temple. In the ever evolving world of Haitian Vodou, there is no perfect answer. Rather, as a religion that is led by the Spirits, they themselves choose their colors and how they wish their particular servitors to call Them.

Petro is the second portion of a Vodou service, and is considered the more intense segment. As we transition out of the Rada segment with the Ogoun family, we sing to the Kongo clan with the Toni rele Kongo refrain:

> *Toni rele Kongo, Toni rele Kongo,*
> *Toni rele Kongo, Santa Marie gracia*

> *Toni calls the Kongo, Toni calls the Kongo,*
> *Toni calls the Kongo, By the grace of Saint Mary*

The origin of this refrain comes directly out of the Kongo history. The Kongo King Anthony was killed at the Battle of Bwila. His descendant, Gangan Kimpa Vita started a movement to re-unify the Kongo people, in order to heal the many rifts that had occurred from all the years of war. Gangan Kimpa Vita became a prophet and in 1704, she began the Toni Malo movement, which threatened the ruling families at the time as well as undermining the authority of the missionaries in the Kongo. When we sing this refrain, we too, are calling all the Kongo to come together in the peristyle for service.[55] It is of note that we sing this verse in kreyol but end in Portuguese, the same language that Toni Malo spoke as well. These glimpses of language are the clues left behind in the Priye that help us understand the roots of the religion via the nations of Africa.

The Lwa called here in the Petro portion originate both in Africa (such as Ogoun) and in the New World (such as Dantor). A very few others who don't fit logically elsewhere (meaning, we don't know their origin, such as Don Pedro), are also called here.

The Petro rites are an interesting mix of elements. In the Petro segment of service, we find things like the tcha-tcha which has a Native American origin, working along with African elements like the nation names of Kita, Zoklimo and Wangol. The majority of detail is derived from the Kongo nation, which as I stated earlier made up more than 50% of the African population.

The native Haitian Lwa reflect their Amerindian attributes. For example, there is the Kowanabo, a lineage of Taino Indian spirits who are maintained through service in the North of Haiti[56].

Ezili Dantor is currently being studied as possibly having a Native American root. Ti Jean Petro is also being studied as a

---

[55] Thornton, J. (1998). *The Kongo Saint Anthony: Dona Beatriz Kimpa Vita and the Antonian Movement, 1684-1706.* New York:Cambridge University Press.
[56] http://www.erzulies.com/site/articles/view/9, accessed 8/2/2010

Native American spirit whose knowledge of native healing plants may be a clue as to his origin or tribal affiliation. Mercedes Foucard Guignard claims that Gran Ibo is none other than Queen Anacaona of the Taino Indians, who gave shelter to maroon slaves and paid for it with her life. Her symbol, the large soup tureen backed with flags is a secret that demonstrates her inclusiveness of the many Africans who found refuge in her mountain camps.[57]

There are other elements in Petro services that harkens back to the island element of the rites. Whistles play a role in calling down the Petro spirits during service. Certain Lwa are very fond of the whistle and will commandeer it as soon as they arrive. Instead of speaking, they use the whistle to signal what they want and who they wish to see. The whistle in effect, becomes their voice. Along with the tch-tcha or maraca, it is one of the prime tools for calling the Petro Lwa into service.

It has been said that the main difference in style between Rada and Petro is one of inner and outer symbols. One of the clearest examples of this, is the asson or beaded rattle that is the emblem of priesthood. The asson is used to call the Rada Lwa into service. The other is the tcha-tcha, used specifically for calling down Petro Lwa.

Rachel Beauvoir Dominique has postulated that the tcha-tcha has it is origins with the Taino Indians. Perhaps the Taino did give the asson to Vodou, but the use of an indigenous plant to

---

[57] Guignard, M.F. (2006). *Les Loa*. Miami, FL: ReMe Art Publishing.

manufacture the instrument is not necessarily the reason. Holy items and delicate objects of the sort like an asson would not have survived the Middle Passage. Africans were pressed to re-invent much of their material culture from resources that were available to them in the new world. The bead-covered gourd called a shekere is African. It is possible that Africans in Saint Domingue adapted an indigenous plant that made a good substitute for what they used back home. Etymologist Pierre Anglade traces the word "ason" to the fongbe "ase".[58] The tcha-tcha as used in Petro rites and characterized by an attached handle and seeds or pellets inside, more likely came from the Taino, who used an instrument just like it which they called "maraka."

I have often thought that as the asson wears its beads on the outside, and is used in Rada services, it demonstrates its origin as being from Africa. The tcha-tcha wears the beads on the inside and is used in Petro services, which have their origins on the island of Haiti. What struck me was the idea of being either "in" or "out", and having this symbol of the beads as a sign post of that direction. I have often said that Vodou is coded. Know the code and you can 'read' the hidden meanings in altars, peristyles, houmfort and even the tap-taps that are so ubiquitous in all of Haiti.

Outward movement - away from Africa (via slavery) is shown by the outer embellishment of the asson, the beaded rattle

---

[58] Anglade, P. (1998). *Inventaire Etymologique des Termes Creoles des Caraibes d'origine Africaine.* Paris: L'Harmattan,.

of priesthood carried by asogwe rank mambos and houngans. Su Pwens also carry the asson, but they are said to be "borrowing" it from their mambo or houngan, as they are in training. Assons are covered with a sort of 'macramé' netting of string, on which are set glass beads and snake vertebrae. As the mambo shakes it, the netting "shusses" over the hard gourd at its core, making a very distinctive rattle sound.

Inward movement was demonstrated by the maroonage of the slaves from the very beginning of the island. Maroonage is the idea of running away, into the interior of the island, into the mountains, to hide in and amongst the native tribes - who also were hiding from the Spanish of the day. The symbolism of the tcha-tcha which carries its beads or seeds on the inside, is the prefer instrument for working Petro style. The Petro rites which include Kongo, Ibo and other tribes, as well as having native influences and names, is all about the interior of the work. It is the inward movement of the work - island based, hidden, secretive - that has as its symbol the hidden sound of the tcha-tcha, also known musically as a maraca. This inward and outward movements, of both sounds and symbols, are excellent examples of the work in Vodou itself.

Public ceremonies, such as the inclusive Rada rites, join the communities they are set in, share in the communion of possession and embrace all who come to dance under the tonnel. The dances are circular, sensuous and embracing. The outer beaded mesh of the asson announces this movement with its susurrus of sound, expressing its power and it is energy through a gentle roll of the hand. The energy is uplifting, communal, and participatory. The "outer" expression of blessings is apparent through the dances, songs and movements of the hounsi choir.

Private work, excluding the community at times and focused on magic is the province of the Petro style. The dances are upright, abrupt, often performed as singular movements, although the dancers appear to move in a group. They are solo interpretations, with each dancer in opposition to the other. The gentle, "outer" susurrus of the asson is replaced by the loud, sharp "inner" clack of the tcha-thca. Even the movement to bring forth the sound is sharp - quick thrusting of the instrument with a back and forth hand. The beads, seeds and stones inside the instrument whack against the head piece, producing a bright sharp sound. The energy is fierce, quick and immediate - with a release that is just as startling in its response.

Inner and Outer symbols are the two key elements of Vodou work, that make all the other pieces of the puzzle fit one another. Knowing which movement you are participating in helps the flow of the service move along. Outer drum patterns roll with the asson's sound. The dances and songs echo this pattern of hidden and revealed power. Petro services are sharp, distinct and abrupt, with the drum playing against the voice and the dancers.

Neither one is better than the other. Each style is set for a purpose, with their individual symbols, sounds and movements lifting the work, imbuing it with power and beauty.

Red is the preferred color of the Petro nations - again, with a second color added in for distinction. Military uniforms, field whips and whistles, all the shrill calls of slave times are here in the service of the Petro section.

Drums in a Petro service are bright, sharp and loud in comparison to their deeper voiced Rada cousins. Our tambor plays Petro with sticks, augmenting the bright sound with splashy hits on the metal rims, and with the ogan or metal bell.

The dances in a Petro service differ from their Rada counterparts by being less rolling and smooth. The steps are staccato, with the body held upright, in defiance of the drum beats and the songs. The arms are held up as if ready to fight, the hips stiff and the feet pounding out backward paced patterns.

All is performed counterpoint to the drums and the established patterns of the beats. This seemingly disparate pattern - drums, feet, body, songs - is meant to throw the servitor off balance, allowing the Lwa entry to their horses. It is also the essential pattern of force and form that gives rise to the presence of the great Lwa themselves.

Petro services are marked by bright, insistent drum beats that ceaselessly play a heartbeat far into a night of prayer and songs. Petro rhythms give birth to foot patterns of dance become hypnotic bridges to the otherworld of Lwa even though they are at first, difficult to manage. The upright posture of the dancers at the beginning of a beat eventually gives way to the weight of the spirit riding the performer. The intricate dances and drum patterns for the servitors give way to "heated" spirits with high energy.

The distinctions of cool and hot lead the Western trained mind into thinking there are two very different Lwa served in each category. Again, this is a partial truth. There are specific Lwa for each nation, and some do cross boundaries, as we spoke of with the Ogouns. But the real difference is in the style of service offered to a particular Lwa. There is a Rada service for Legba and a Petro service, too. Legba is Legba, but the manner in which he is served is the manner in which he works for you. The concept of good and bad is a Western modality of identifying spirits. The Vodou Lwa are not divided in this manner. There are just the spirits and the ways in which we, humanity, choose to serve them.

Categorizing Lwa into Rada or Petro is based upon their essential nature at rest. "Cool" refers to greater patience and a calm nature. Most of the Rada Lwa are like family. They are forgiving, easy to negotiate with, slow to temper. This broad category of Lwa are older within the tradition, have been known and worked with for a long time, and so are used to our ways and faults. They are patient with the human servitor who promises them a service, but is waylaid by life and so cannot fulfill the obligation. The Rada Lwa are tolerant of us as we strive to learn and serve them.

"Hot" applies very well to the Petro Lwa. Excluding the Nago nation, the Kreyol Lwa of Haiti are younger and more exacting of their servitors. They are intense, demanding, abrupt in their nature and personalities. They do not have time for laziness, forgetfulness or insolence. They are fast and quick to work, easily offended at broken promises and not at all forgiving for the offense. If you promise Danbala something and don't deliver, he'll just ignore you and keep on doing his thing. If you promise Dantor something and then renege on it, you just might find your car windows blown out on a clear cloudless day.

This is not to say the Lwa are temperamental with a thirst for vengeance. They are not. But just as I always say that the Lwa do not lead our lives for us, the Lwa can just as easily withdraw their protections, their guidance and their inspiration. Inspiration could have prevented the window blow out if I had listened to my inner voice tell me not to park under the tree in front of my house. A sudden windstorm came up and voila – busted car windows.

There is another aspect to the service portion of a Vodou ceremony that I'll call "style." The "style" of Rada is white, cool, calm. Deliberate dances feature the body in supplication, with hands held at the side. Formal is a good word for Rada services.

The style of Petro is red, hot, fast paced. Defiant body postures, staccato drum beats. Revolutionary is the word I use to describe Petro services.

We have friends in the Artibonite Valley and they serve their Lwa in their own unique family style. We compare differences all the time, as we are what is called "Ginen" priests, meaning we keep a Rada house exclusively. They also serve Rada but their main services center on Petro or island Lwa. We find that the major elements of a given service are the same, but the details change the most. We both sing for the Lwa, but not in the same order. We sing for Legba first and they sing for the Marasa first. We serve Kadja Bossou and they serve Djobolo Bossou. Similar services but different expressions.

This difference in style is readily apparent to anyone who visits many houses across the country of Haiti. We have been privileged to serve alongside some of the best houngans and mambos around. Their konnesans is breathtaking and the styles of their services remarkably the same yet different. We all salute Danbala, but some of us salute him with water, some with anisette, some with clarin and anise seed. We all use white cloth to cover him when he arrives. But some of us use a white sheet, while others use white lace. The same yet different. I think this difference may account for the variations in reports by anthropologists of the 30s and 40s who did not truly understand what they were seeing, yet reported everything as "...this is how Vodou is done." This makes for a very confusing set of facts that sometimes conflict with one another.

The best way to understand styles of service is to attend real Vodou services. There is a lot of what I would term 'tourist' Vodou happening and for a price, the performance is often quite good. But real Vodou isn't flashy or touristy. It is quiet, compelling and religious. The songs are vocal codes of pain, adoration and hope. They are sung in soft, plaintive voices calling out for succor and blessings. And the presence of the Divine is seen in the face of the ancient priests who have lived through much and know how uplifting the service can be for those who need it most. The Divine is felt in the touch of the Lwa passing by you. A cheek stroked. The hair lifted off your neck. The frisson of passé as Spirit moves through the crowd. And we see the Divine in the faces of those possessed. It is both awe inspiring and beautiful.

The basic nature of each "style" gives each kind of service its own unique stamp. It lends to the service the look, the sound and the feel of the service. Each has its place and its power. And each is partnered with the other in the dance of the Vodoun.

Chapter Ten: Ceremonies in Vodou

In the last chapter, we spoke about the styles of service that make up the practice we call Vodou. Color, music, dance and rhythm all combine to create a focused intent, that brings about the blessing presence of the Lwa. Like the concentric circles we spoke of, these styles then fit into patterns we call ceremonies.

Ceremonial styles are predicated on a number of factors. First is the intent of the ceremony. As in life, intent in Vodou gives the ceremony a voice, a direction in which the mambo or houngan lead the congregation. A ceremony to celebrate a particular Lwa's feast day would have a very different intent (as well as look and feel) than a ceremony for burying the dead.

The intent of the ceremony gives it the parameters by which everyone can come to a consensus in terms of what kind of energy the ceremony has. A celebration of the Lwa would feature table cloths and flowers in the colors that Lwa enjoys. The food would be the preferences of the celebrated Lwa. And the songs sung would also follow suit. A ceremony for the dead would have white as the dominant color because that is the color of the ancestors. The food would be ancestrally focused such as white bread, black coffee and white pudding. The songs would be appropriate to the working -- mournful, releasing or uplifting depending on the intent of the ceremony. Each ceremony and its participants would benefit from the knowledge that the appropriate paradigms were employed, in order to best serve the purpose and goals of the ceremony itself.

Styles of service in ceremony is a very broad topic, but one that I will attempt to address by the main components as I have experienced them. Many houses follow a cycle of services for particular reasons. The cycle of death is one that comes to mind, with its four main rites of Dessounen, Anba Dlo, Casa Canari and Retire Mo Nan Dlo. But individual Vodou houses also add a variety of improvised details to the regular rituals that all sosyetes and houses share. For instances, a given house may not be able to hold the rites in the set time frame, so they must wait, while money is collected and time accrued. Or they choose to host a service at a different time of year. Or they simply can afford a finer item in place of whatever the Reglemen says is the minimum needed. For many reasons, the variety of ceremonies performed is as varied as the houses that hold them.

It is a truism that there is no "pope" in Vodou. This freedom of expression in service is the guiding principle for all Vodou priests. It can also be an obfuscation for the anthropologist who tries to shoe-horn the ceremonies of Vodou into neat categories. As Vodou includes and does not exclude, it becomes very tough to try and compartmentalize all the various styles, purposes and intentions of the collective Vodou liturgical body. Each house is free to add, subtract or improvise as they see fit, but there are some generalizations that one comes across in the practice of Vodou.

The ceremonies of Vodou mirror the Kongo concept of man having a beginning, middle and an end, with a period of rest. We see this concept in the rituals of baptisms (batems - a beginning), kanzos and lave tets (middle), and the rituals of death (ending), particularly the Anba Dlo and Casa Canari.

Because Vodou is entwined with Roman Catholicism, it takes parts of that religion and fuses it with Vodou's own needs and desires. The calendar of observances in Vodou is entwined with the Catholic one. For example, Vodou observes the Epiphany or Three Kings Day for the Simbis. For the non-Catholic readers, the three Kings were holy Magi. The Kings association with the Simbis is due to their perceived magical abilities which they share with the Simbi nachon.

Vodou honors the Lenten season with a ceasing of services, in observance of the 40 day fast of Christ. And Vodou uses the various saint feast days as the feast days of the Lwa they are synchronized with. Vodou also follows the major holidays such as Easter and Christmas by adding its own touches to both holidays. Resurrection services are held at Easter and special bathes and lave tets are done at Christmas.

All Vodou ceremonies begin with your name, which is really the first magically protective formula you receive in the faith. Naming ceremonies are very important within the African traditional religions. The value of two names has an inner meaning in terms of magic and mythology. Knowing someone's true name is a means of controlling them. Often, a child was given a secret family name, known only to those closest to them. This was considered their true name because it represented them in their truest form. They were also given a "public" name that anyone could call them by, but it was less powerful in terms of meaning and mythology within the family. Names of deceased relatives or family surnames were often the public name, passed from generation to generation. We have a trace memory of this, in the popularity of naming kids after grandparents or great-uncles and great aunts.

Anyone who has a secret family knows the value of this dual identity strategy. I have two names – a public one (Patricia) and a family one, that I keep for those folks who know me well. When I am in a public place or at a gathering, I can tell who knows me very well by the name they call me by. And by association, those who use my 'family' name are known to one another as well.

It was much the same for the Ancestors, who answered to their "slave" names in the field, but kept their "real" names as power points within the family. This same strategy is applied in Vodou. Initiates are given a nom vayan or 'valiant name' at their naming services. The Ancestors knew the value of this, and were cautious to give names that upheld and encouraged a child. Names were often mottos, such as a title or praise name for the Lwa. My nom vanyan is Bon Mambo Vye Zo Komande La Menfo Daginen. It means "Old Bones Commands with a Strong Hand of Ginen," and it is a praise name of Legba. A name was and still is something for the child to grow into, uplifting them and inspiring them to great achievements. It is the same for *nom vayans* in Vodou.

Naming ceremonies in Haiti today are still considered the first rite of passage for a child in the world. In a country where new mothers often do not name their babies for three months (out of fear that the child will die), the name conferred upon a newborn is of utmost importance. It is the same for the Vodouisant.

Names are conferred with a Batem or baptism for both newborns and older folks into Vodou. Much as a Catholic baptism has godparents who stand for the baby, Vodou is the same. In Vodou, we bring the new convert a set of guiding mentors who we name "God parents". The male is called in kreyol *Parinn* and the female is called *Marinn*.

At the time of birth a baby is given these folks as their spiritual guides to help foster them through the world into new places and new ideas, new ways of thinking. The ritual of baptism for a newborn is a simple lave tet. The newborn is held by the godparents as the mambo washes the baby's feet, preparing her to be able to walk in the world. Then mambo pours a tiny bit of water over the baby's head to help start the baby off with a cool level head, always the goal of any Vodouisant.

Finally, the baby is given a tiny taste of salt so that she will know the bitter of life, followed by a finger wet with wine to taste the sweet. Prayers are offered to the Ancestors who are expected to walk with the child and to offer protection as well as guidance. The baby is then named and wrapped in a cloth that is kept for the duration of her life. This name is her "public" name, the one she will be known by when others speak of her. The newborn will also have a private name used only among the immediate family and her spirits. In time she will gain several others as well.[59]

For older people, who choose to come into Vodou as adults, these godparents have the added plus of what is known as konnesans or spiritual knowledge. The idea is that the godparents have been in the faith for a period of time and can offer guidance, explanations and comfort to the new hunyo or spirit child. These adults also have their heads washed, but it is a much more involved ritual called a Lave Tet.

LAVE TET

Lave Tets are perhaps the most widely performed ritual of Vodou. Each house, again, has its own methodology on how they achieve their results. The basic service is to mix a bath of clean water with fresh herbs that are pertinent to the result desired. Lave Tets can be performed as cleansing actions, purification rites or re-balancing ceremonies. Some Lave Tets heal an emotional

---

[59] Branche, A. (2005). *African Initiations: Rites of Passage through the eyes of an Initiate.* Philadelphia, PA: Borders Personal Publishing.

pain. Other heal physical ones. And then there are spiritual lave tets that heal the soul, so that the person is placed in balance with their spirits and ancestors. Lave Tets are the secret knowledge of mambos and houngans. The formulas, herbs, perfumes and oils added to a bath mixture are kept secret by the priests. Successful formulas are never given out, but handed down from priest to initiate as inner knowledge of the temple.

Most often a person undergoes a lave tet to begin their spiritual journey toward balance and understanding. Vodou is all about healing. Healing spiritually, emotionally and mentally. It is the outward goal of Vodou to maintain inner equilibrium at all times. A cool head is a preferred state of being. It allows one to think clearly and to make rational decisions. A Lave Tet can often help a person realize that goal for themselves. It is also the baptism into the faith of Vodou.

Lave Tets properly should be done as an overnight event. The participant is confined to the peristyle proper where they can begin to recede within themselves and prepare for change. It is always preferable to have the participant on the same page as the Mambo when working for a specific goal. This is facilitated with prayers, songs and drum beats. In some temples, modern practices such as meditation and pathworking have begun to be employed as tools to help facilitate the correct state of being for the participant.

We open Sosyete du Marche's Lave Tet ritual with the Priye Ginen, and then request the participants to change out of their street clothing. They change into old clothing which will be tossed after the service. This signifies an end to their old behaviors and allows a new pattern to begin. The participants are bathed with an infusion of fresh green herbs from our gardens. We grow all our own herbs and handpick everything the morning of the Lave Tet. We sing, we drum and we dance hard to create the correct vibration for the participant, so they will receive the correct energy for their goals. Often the Lwa themselves arrive and refine the bath with additional things. We keep a huge array of perfumes, lotions, essential oils and tinctures on hand so the Lwa may pick and choose as they wish.

After the physical lave is performed, the participants change into new, dry clothing. We wrap them in clean sheets and put them to bed for the night. In the morning, we host an Action de Gras or act of thanks for the Lwa's blessings and participation. Once completed, the participant is free to go home. Folks have told me that they feel free, as if they put down a large suitcase that they had been carrying without knowing what it contained. A lave tet at its best allows the participant to feel different when completed.

Lave Tets are also done as an introduction to a Vodou house. Some people do not wish to make a deep connection until they have had time to process the many changes they will experience in service. For these folks, a lave tet is often a great opportunity to commit in a more personal manner, allowing them time to get acclimated to the house, its membership and its method of working.

Finally, a Lave Tet can be done multiple times for particularly tough issues. It is not uncommon to perform a Lave Tet over a period of three, five or seven days, with multiple baths, divinatory readings and rituals all crafted toward a specific purpose. Spirit attachments, prolonged illnesses, melancholy and depression all benefit from extended forms of Lave Tet. Each house creates this ritual for the individual receiving the bath. But the basics are always the same. If at all possible, fresh green herbs are used. The participant is allowed a time of "kouche" in order to allow the benefits of the Lave to enter their limbic system. And each participant is expected to experience a change in their lives from their submersion in the bath waters.

Building on the service of naming, we also find that it plays a role in some of the life ceremonies of Vodou as well. Furthering a candidate's abilities in life, in service and in spiritually are all part of moving forward in the Vodou faith. One can begin the journey of a lifetime with one step, and that first step into Vodou is a Lave Tet or the extended Sevis Tet. Today, these ceremonies have become the most widely performed ones by sosyetes both here and in Haiti. The Lave Tet is done for balancing, healing, or a general cleansing.

SEVIS TET

Lave Tets are the opening ritual for the cycle of services in our house that we call Sevis Tet or "Service of the Head". This is a three or five day affair (depending on the house), conferring the title of Hounsi Bossale, and creating a deep, spiritual bond between the candidate and the house or sosyete that they join. Offered as a first step on to the path of the Vodou religion, it holds an important place in the overall make up of the candidate's spiritual life. Sevis Tet aligns the person to the energies of the house they are working or serving in. It gives them a small taste of the rigors of service and makes the initial contact with one's self that is so important in all the ATRs. Knowledge of oneself is at the heart of African Traditional Religions. As part of that knowledge a new name signifies a change in perception and character for the individual.

KANZO

The Lave Tet is also a part of a large cycle of rituals called Kanzo. These are the initiatory rites where mambos, houngans and hounsis are created. The Lave Tet is the opening ritual within that cycle and confers cleanliness and coolness to the candidate. It is interesting to note that the concentric circles of Vodou also have a place with the rituals performed in Vodou. Lave Tet is contained with the Kanzo cycle. And the Kanzo cycle is also a concentric set of rituals. All these rituals are created to bring the candidate closer to the Divine through prayer, meditation, herbal application and homeopathic application of plants and leaves.

Kanzo begins with the 21 baths of dissolution. These baths are crafted to help you leave the life you have for the one you want. The 21 baths are given over a period of one day, as the candidates sit in consignee (confinement), awaiting their moment to enter the holy djevo. In Sosyete du Marche, we brew our own herbal waters for use in the Kanzo. Called hydrosols, they are aromatically infused with the herb's essential oils and properties. Combined with clean water, fresh herbs, perfume, alcohol and essential oils combine to create an amazing sensory experience. Once the baths are complete, the candidate is considered a "mo" or a dead, and is kept from view from the living. Like the Kalunga of the Kongo, the living and the dead do not cohabitate.

The candidates are then brought into the djevo with song and prayer and a long night of dancing. This is the Chire Ayizan, the purifying dance that cleanses the djevo, making it ready for the candidates to enter. The djevo is the womb of Ayizan, the mother of the kanzos, and none may pass who are not prepared to commit to her for life. A beautiful ceremony, the Chire Ayizan is performed with pomp and circumstance, as the candidates are brought in, and bedded down for their kouche.

The rest is secret and cannot be divulged. There are rituals performed, oaths given and many secret teachings that will empower the candidate for their new life as a kanzo.

The final night in the djevo, the hunyos (the spirit children, a name for the candidates of kanzo) are taken out and put through the Brule Zin or fire walk of the ancestors. Having been tested in the djevo, they are ready to prove they are invincible with Spirit. The fires of the Ancestors are lit up and the hunyos are put to the test. If they pass, they are considered Kanzo – literally Fire Bones, the toughest and hardest passage of all.

Following the Brule Zin, is the Batem, where the candidates rise with the dawn and are baptized with new names. They are assigned godparents to help mentor them through their new lives, and are given all the tools required to live as Vodou initiates, practicing their faith and serving their spirits.

Kanzo is community at its best. The community comes out to see the newly consecrated initiates pass their tests and to cheer them on. What begins with a simple Lave Tet to cleanse, balance and purify, rises to become the Holy Kanzo, the biggest and most important ceremony for the living.

Kanzo is a large and serious undertaking. The three ranks of Kanzo -- Hounsi Kanzo, Su Pwen and Asogwe -- all involve oaths and promises of service to the spirits. Hounsi Kanzo is the entry level rank, making the person a formal servitor of a given sosyete. Hounsis are the backbone of a Vodou house. These are the people who are most often the horse of the Lwa and who work to help keep a given sosyete running smoothly. Su Pwen is the entry level of priesthood. Here the initiate learns to serve the spirits more fully by helping the Asogwe leader of the house in their tasks. Those tasks include singing the Priye or leading songs; performing services such as Lave Tets; learning all the details of running a beautiful ceremony for the Lwa. The Asogwe rank is the highest. The person who receives this rank is a formal priest of Vodou and promises to be of service to the community, to run ceremonies for the public and to hold services for the house membership as well as their spiritual and physical families. These then are the ranks of kanzo and they are all consuming in their obligations, their function and their expression in the world. A Kanzo candidate makes promises on their final day of confinement that must be kept or else they risk offending the spirits. But there is another ritual that confers a special grace, though it does not confer priesthood.

MARAJ LWA: A SPIRITUAL UNION

The Maraj Lwa has also become a naming ceremony, of a kind. It is the most popular ceremony held here in the US, following the Kanzo. A maraj is performed when a Lwa asks to be wed to their favorite servitor.

At times, it becomes obvious that a Spirit has a particular interest in someone. They manifest repeatedly at services, and spend time with a person, talking to them, sharing insights and offering advice. When the spirit deems it necessary, They will request to marry a given individual. Marriage with the Spirits follows certain protocols. Male spirits can marry men, as females can marry women. And of course, the sexes do mix. I feel that the Spirits assume the roles that we give them. Is Ogoun really a man? I rather doubt it. Ogoun is a huge spiritual dimension, encompassing more than just war and strife, but restless energy, health and physicality, strategy and power. That we choose to envision this incredible vast energy as simply male is all our little human minds can hold. Ogoun is everything we make of him and much, much more. Hence, he can marry anyone he pleases!

A Maraj Lwa should only be performed when the spirit requests it. And even then, the best way to ascertain the truth of the request is to ask the spirit to wait for a period of time, while you decide. If the spirit acquiesces to the request, then you can be fairly certain the request is real, and the presiding priest will begin negotiating with that spirit for the terms of your marriage, including the name by which they wish to be known to you, and you, to them.

I say this because there are stray spirits who often pose as Lwa. These spirits are very attached to the sensate life they had and will do anything to get back to that life, even it it's just receiving offerings. The unsuspecting individual who signs on for a marriage sometimes find themselves saddled with impossible responsibilities and a spirit who is less than willing to help or work with them. When this happens, you can be sure the marriage was not made with the Lwa but with a stray "mo'" or dead spirit who pretended to be the Lwa. The results can range from a cantankerous entity who keeps you up at night making noises, to a dangerous and potentially harmful spirit who drains you emotionally and physically through depression, melancholy and pathos. Be sure of whom you are working with before doing anything like a maraj!

But for this discussion, let us say you have determined that the Lwa is who they say they are and you are happily planning your marriage to them. The mambo will help make the arrangements for the wedding. It can be as lavish or as simple as you wish it to be. There will be a contract, negotiated ahead of time, detailing your relationship with the Lwa. It can run the gamut from a single night of service to an elaborate month of parties and ceremonies. Sometimes, the Lwa wish to spend time with you. You might need to sleep alone on the night of your marriage or the night of the Lwa, so they may come to you in dreams. You could prepare a room for say Erzulie, all in pink. The bed linens are smooth, super crisp and white. There are fresh roses in a vase, and the room is perfumed with rose water. You dress in pink, tie your head with a pink mushoir and go to sleep, so that Erzulie will come and speak with you in your dreams. You might do this one night a week, or one night a month, or one night a year. It is all in the marriage contract, worked out ahead of time with the Mambo and the Lwa.

Once you have the contract set, the wedding ceremony begins. The Lwa arrive and their horse stands with you, as the contract is read out loud to the congregation. You both sign it, and witnesses come forward to see that all is in order. Then, you exchange rings. If you marry Erzulie, be prepared to buy her the very best you can afford. If you marry Ogoun, an iron horseshoe nail would be very appropriate. You can use your imagination. The ring should evoke the Lwa and their signature energy. And you will wear it just as you would a regular wedding ring: with pride, with purpose and with love.

The Lwa love their servitors. They work hard to be here with us. Everything in a ceremony, from the flowers to the food to the songs is employed to call forth the Mysteries for our own benefit as well as theirs. And the benefits of having the Lwa present are seen in all the various services we do with and for them. These ceremonies are all about living with the Lwa here and now. But the living are not the only ones who benefit from the many ceremonies of Vodou.

For those who have died, the rites and services continue to support the idea of a family centric paradigm. When a person dies, there are a series of ceremonies held to assure that person's place in the afterlife. They are called the Dessounen, the Anba Dlo (Bohoun), Retire Mo nan Dlo and the Casa Canari.

DESSOUNEN

The Dessounen refers to the rites of separation performed when someone has died. In Vodou theology, the Ti-Bon Anj (Little Good Angel) is the will of the person which returns to stand before God, recounting the life just lived. The Gros Bon Anj (Big Good Angel) is the animating force of the body. When the body dies, it must be properly separated from the body and given a chance to rest in the Immortal Waters of Return. There, it unites with the community of Ancestral Dead, and rests from its earthly travails.

The work of taking down the metaphysical bonds of the body requires long hours of prayer and song. This effort sets the

Met Tet free to choose whether to remain earth bound or return to the heaven or even become another person's Lwa. The Dessounen is performed ideally when the body is dying, but as often as not it is done after the death.

As the body lies in state, the priest calls together the family to witness the rite. With water and asson, he sings over the body, calling and enticing the Lwa to leave the servitor and rejoin the family. I have said that the Lwa love their servitors. We are not the only ones who grieve when a person dies. The energy that has walked with them their entire life weeps as well. It often takes time for the Lwa to accept that their servitor has passed on, leaving behind an empty shell. It is the job of the mambo or houngan to help the Lwa realize that life has ended and they need to move on as well. when Mambo Celanie Constant Nerva passed away in Jacmel, Haiti, a dozen houngans assembled to sing for her spirits because there were so many heavy with sadness at her passing.[60]

Once the Lwa have been called forth, they sometimes choose someone to be with. That person is usually a member of the immediate family and they accept the Lwa as a Racine spirit who will walk with them, and help them, as the Lwa has helped the servitor. Other times, the Lwa decides that they will return to the Godhead and invest their knowledge and konnesans into the

---

[60] *Communication with Houngan R Morse in Port-au-Prince, 2009.*

greater good of Humanity. With special prayers, offerings and drum beats, the Dessounen is the first rite of death for the Servitor.

ANBA DLO (ALSO KNOWN AS THE BOHOUN)

This particular ritual has seen a re-emergence since the earthquake. Many groups either hosted a Bohoun or performed it for the community as a way of healing the pain of death and offering closure to those who lost family and friends in the disaster. Sometimes, this ritual is done along with the Dessounen, so that as the Lwa leaves, the Gros Bon Ange of the person is placed in the Abysmal Waters of return. Other times it is offered as a community rite of passage, to help heal those who mourn the death of others.

The sosyete gathers around two or more casa canari jars that are placed into large kivets, so they float on water. As the sosyete sings, the hounsis beat upon the floating canari jars with wooden mallets. The object is to break the jars, symbolically freeing the soul from its body of clay. This ritual frees the Gros Bon Ange to dissipate and return to the earth. Once the jars break, the body is washed, dressed and buried. The broken jars and water from the kivets are taken to the nearest crossroads and tossed into the center, placing them within the domain of Legba. As the guardian who can open the way to Heaven for the deceased, Legba can return the spirit of the person to the place of the ancestors. The sosyete returns to the peristyle to sing and celebrate the life of the deceased, much as a wake is done here in the US. The death rites completed, the family falls into mourning.

RETIRE MO NAN DLO

After a period of time has passed, the family gathers again to participate in the Retire Mo Nan Dlo, the taking of the Gros Bon Ange out of the waters and placing them into a canari jar, also known as a govi. This ritual is not performed very often. Elaborate and expensive, the Retire Mo is a piece of history that is slowly but surely fading away.

Large and elaborate jars are marked out with symbols, vèvès and call signs. The houngan/mambo sets up a tent and the hounsi lay with just their heads inside the tent, the canari jars lined up on the earth, against their heads. The houngan/mambo calls up the dead person and requests that they reside within the canari. Here they are served their favorite foods and drinks. When the houngan/mambo is convinced the spirits are in the canaries, the jars are passed over the sacred fires of a brule zin, in order to warm the spirit and get them ready to work.

After completion of the Brule Zin, the jars are then placed on the family ancestral altar, where they sit receiving food and drink, and can offer the family advice and consolation for all kinds of matters. We see this remembrance in things like the egun (ancestor) pots of the Yoruba and the ancestral butsudans[61] of the Japanese. In Haiti, it is the sacred govis that hold the many ancestral spirits that one can work and walk with.

CASA CANARI

The final ritual of death is called Casa Canari[62] and it is seldom performed any longer in Haiti, though we do hold Casa Canari from time to time for our beloved ancestors. After a long period of mourning, the family may choose to release the Gros Bon Ange from its terrestrial resting place, so that it may return to the Divine. The canari jar containing its Gros Bon Ange is placed in a large pan of water. With prayers, songs and drum beats, the hounsi gather round and beat on the clay vessel with heavy wood sticks, until it shatters. This is not an easy feat. These jars are heavy, thick clay and do not break easily. With continual beating the vessels eventually shatter. The pieces are quickly gathered and taken to the crossroads where the water and broken vessel are scattered. The sosyete returns home and finishes the service with song and dance. The vessel has released the soul to return to the Divine.

These are the major services of Vodou. There are many others. Each region of Haiti has differences in service style, songs and drum beats. When we were at Saut d'Eau one year, we sang for

---

[61] *http://en.wikipedia.org/wiki/Butsudan*, accessed 2011
[62] *http://www.ht.refer.org/OMR/_regions/cass-kan_dah-1.htm*, accessed 2009

Danbala. The assembled crowd politely listened. Then one man stepped forward and sang the same song to me, but with a completely different melody. I often compare song melodies with other servitors and we continually find both similarities in song structure, but often major differences in melodies and harmonies. Ceremonies are similar to this. Attend a ceremony for Ogoun at three different houses and you will see, hear and experience three very different rites. The structure of the night will seem similar, but different, in the way each set of priests chooses to add or subtract from the basic service. But in the end, the Lwa Ogoun is served and every one present at each, is blessed by His ashe.

You cannot help but be moved by a beautiful service. The music, the songs and the sense of inclusiveness is at the heart of what makes a service so wonderful. This inclusiveness is also what makes the service so rewarding. The Lwa do not differentiate between the people at a service. They choose us all because Vodou includes; it does not exclude.

Chapter Eleven: Possession and Sacrifice

The two most inflammatory topics within religion of Vodou are most certainly possession and sacrifice. I cannot remember if I have ever spoken publicly where those two topics were not the first questions asked. "What about possession?" is the usual inquiry, followed by "Do you kill chickens?". The answers may surprise you

Possession is the sacrament of Vodou. It is the preferred state of being for those are participating in a Vodou service. It is through the grace of possession that we find communion with the Divine and His messengers, the Lwa. But you might be surprised to hear me say that possession is not necessary to a successful service. In fact, real possession is a rare and beautiful event, and does not always happen as you might expect.

Maya Deren wrote the definitive description of a possession state[63]. She called it "the white darkness" and likened it to falling down into a deep space within yourself, where time and light become one, only to be recalled back to this present time in an instant. I think that's a fair description.

What happens when a possession state is reached? It is different for everyone. You will find some people say that only a

---

[63] Deren, M. (1953). *Divine Horsemen*, New York: Vanguard Press.

total blank, a complete lack of the memory is a true possession. Others will say they had an 'inkling' of what was going on around them. Overall, the consensus is that possession is a state of being where you recede and the Lwa come forward. That recession can be partial or total, depending on your comfort level.

A partial possession is referred to as a passé, meaning the spirit passed you by. You know this because perhaps the hair on your arm stood up or you had goose bumps suddenly. You might become momentarily dizzy, but you remained aware of your surroundings. Sometimes, you can experience numbness in your legs or arms, but that is all that happened. In our house, these are all good signs that you were found interesting by the Lwa. They touched you briefly, and it is a welcome sign of their presence.

A total possession means your head was taken by a Lwa and you have no memory of the event. By taken, I mean that one moment, you were dancing and the next you are sitting on a chair with red and blue scarves on your arms, a machete in one hand, a bottle of rum in the other and no idea how that came to be. The people around you nod, saying Papa Ogoun said this or Ogoun did that. But you don't remember anything let alone a man named Ogoun. That is what a total possession state feels like. There's a literal blank in your mind or memory.

I tell my students a true possession is disconcerting at best and downright frightening at worse. And what I mean is that when I am ready for it to happen, I can gracefully exit my consciousness, feeling confident that when the Lwa are done with me I will return, no harm done. But sometimes, I return to this present state in a place of anxiety and exhaustion. The latter most often happens when an entity I am not knowledgeable about catches me off guard and takes my head. As a mambo asogwe, it is my duty to serve the community. Sometimes, I err on letting things into my mind that are not exactly on speaking terms with my own spirits. And when that happens, I find the experience less than pleasant.

And therein lies the answer to total, partial or none at all states of possession. I teach this part to all our students. You are in control at all times. I do not go in for the 'devil made me do it' scenario. Either you want to let it happen, or you do not. It's that simple. If you want to let it happen, it will. These are spirits that move through time and space incorporeally. They can certainly move into you as well. So either you choose to allow them to come forward and take you totally or not at all. But you make the rules. It is through your willingness that possession can occur. Don't want to have it happen? It will not, and you most likely will have passé. Desire the alliance and it might happen or it might not. It's really the Lwa's choice, not ours. We can merely be receptive to the event. The Lwa choose who they will.

The idea of a total possession is at the heart and soul of the work in a Vodou service. We want the Lwa to come down and give us their blessing. To do that, they must possess someone. So the unspoken question is "if the Lwa come into me, where do I go?" The answer is nowhere. You are the animating force of your body. Your consciousness must remain in some way, in order to help control your body. Tom Cowan, the Celtic Shaman who teaches the Michael Harner method of Shamanism, talks about the 2% consciousness that remains behind when the shaman undertakes a journey. That 2% keeps the body breathing, and is responsible for allowing the shaman to return. I feel that much the same thing takes place during a possession state. Some tiny part of our consciousness must remain in order for the body to function and the space to be held open for the mind to return. However, that does not mean you remember everything. It means that you are safe to allow those spirits known to you to be in an intimate embrace with you. That is the first point of possession. Possession states are most often known spirits. In occult circles, we call it "Knowledge and Conversation of Your Holy Guardian Angel." Your Spirits would never harm you, and so they are the ones most likely to step into your mind in order to offering healing or advise to the community (and you by proxy).

There is another point that gets missed in the discussion of possessions and that is "Why can't I get possessed by myself?" Well, first off, who would be there to validate the event? If you are alone, then no one can vouch for the state of grace. Solo possession states are the quickest way to madness in my thinking. I feel that the ego that needs to declare this is not a fit vessel for the ashe in the first place.

I also teach that the Lwa are morally neutral entities. They are not human nor were they ever as far as I know. We cannot expect them to adhere to our human value system. Therefore, it is only prudent to approach them with great care, loads of respect and a good dose of caution. Meaning, one doesn't go setting up an altar to the Lwa on Saturday night to get possessed for the fun of it. These same entities have been fetted and served a specific way for a millennium and with good reason. It isn't just for the purpose of keeping them happy but to *protect ourselves from them*. Remember the rules of propitiation. Service to the gods was to keep them in their own plane of existence so they would not cause havoc by coming into ours. If you call up Ezili Freda without the proper protocols, you might be surprised at who comes knocking at your door and what occurs in the arrival.

Possession by these supra entities then begins to take on a different tone when viewed in this light. One doesn't want to be the chosen vessel so much as be the audience for the vessel's spirit. If you are the vessel, then you don't get to hear the message, receive the blessings or even ask the Lwa something. As the audience, you are in place to receive everything the Lwa bring to the fet. When viewed in this light, we can see that being the vessel is a personal sacrifice for the community. The person who undergoes possession is the one who is left behind (literally) to be the upholder of the energy for the rest of the community.

We do work to bring about possession in our services. But the Asogwe rank is the person who is the vessel. That is because their head has been properly prepared to receive the Lwa. They have been tempered by fire into a vessel that can hold the flame of heaven safely. And in doing so, they become the crucible formed by the Lwa, for the community to drink from. That is the second point of possession. Communion with the Lwa for the entire community, not one person.

A solo possession state is viewed as selfish, self centered and egotistical. A community possession state is selfless, outwardly focused and egoless. The Lwa choose their vessel accordingly. And always, for the purpose of community healing.

The vessel that holds the spirit is not as important as the presence of the spirit themselves. This last bit has gotten lost in recent practice. I continually hear about possessions where the vessel expects to be treated as someone special because they were possessed. This is culturally insensitive to the work of Vodou which is about balancing community relations. It carries a morally skewed outlook about possessions and their intended purpose. Being the vessel is not the point of the exercise. Hearing the message is the real reason for allowing the spirits to be present in the first place. When we remember this, then the possession is clean, the message is clear, the community as a whole is healed and balance is restored.

I mentioned sacrifice earlier in this chapter. Sacrifice in Vodou is also a very big touch point. In this country, we have become unaware of the work involved in creating food for the masses. As a child of the seashore, I was inducted into the work of cleaning and skinning my own food at an early age. When the fish ran at the shore, all able bodied folks went to work to take in what we could for our families. I learned early how humane killing was done and not to waste life without a purpose.

Sacrifice in Vodou is done both with intent and with purpose. Life is precious and nowhere more so than in Haiti. Animals are an expensive commodity and they are not dispatched with impunity for just any reason. Some families save up for years, in order to make the correct offerings for family services. When that much thought and effort in placed in a purchase, the animal in question is gratefully cared for, until it is needed.

People living in Haiti do not have the advantage of shopping for a meal in a near-by grocery store. Most often dinner was wandering around the lakou, before it ended up on the table. Living closer to the land, practicing animal husbandry, caring for the very thing that gives you sustenance, makes you appreciate its life all the more.

When ceremonies are held, it is expected that the presiding priest will provide a meal to everyone who is in attendance. That could mean feeding forty people or a hundred. For a large celebration, it can mean feeding folks for a couple days. Many animals may be needed: to make stew, to make offerings and to feed the crowds that come to watch and participate. These animals are blessed; offered with intent to the Lwa; are dispatched quickly; are cleaned, dressed, cooked and served to everyone who has come to the peristyle. Remember, it is the tropics. Food can spoil very quickly, so the entire animal is used and nothing is wasted. An animal blessed and consecrated, killed humanely and then served to the community makes more sense to me than a slaughter house product in a plastic container.

Sacrifice is only performed for certain rituals, and is not a regular practice in Haiti or in our house. No one but an experienced priest should attempt to do a live sacrifice of any kind, for any reason. You can reap more problems than you realize, from breaking local ordinances, to offering the wrong animal to the wrong spirit. There are hundreds of ways to make an offering to the Lwa that do not involve taking a life. Those are the ones that should be followed with humility and care. The rest should be left to those priests skilled in such disciplines in Vodou.

Chapter Twelve: Where do I go from here?

This book was not meant to be a complete tutorial on all you need to know about Vodou. No book can do that (not even this one.) Rather, it is a guide, a starting point. No one can learn all there is to know about Vodou from any one source. There is even a proverb in Haiti that says: "Ki tan ou bezwen jwenn, epi ale jwenn." It means, whatever you need to find, go and find." It is an allusion to the fact that no one person has all the knowledge. We need to work with many people to gain our konnesans. In this way, we not only find our place with the elders, but we respect the tradition by honoring those elders' knowledge.

A reputable house will train its membership, so that when they visit other sosyetes they make a good impression. It is a sign of how well the servitor is made. When our membership visits another house, their behavior is a direct reflection on my own abilities as a mambo. If the ti-fey ('little leaves' meaning servitors of this house) demonstrate their konnesans by correct behavior in service, then they are seen as having been given correct instruction. The unspoken part is that I as their Mambo am also giving correct service to the Lwa. It is all interrelated.

Vodou is a living religion. It means that the Lwa are very involved in their services. They constantly give us new details, new songs, new *langaj* to speak with them. This involvement with their servitors gives Vodou its fresh, up to the date feel. We can always count on the Lwa to help us when we are stuck in a rut.

The theology and liturgy of Vodou constantly evolves. It is what drew me to Vodou in the first place. The freshness of the liturgy, the constant and steady evolution of its theology, the direct involvement of the spirits all spoke to a path that was current and modern. Yet, at the same time, it gave great respect and honor to the past. I now know why. It is all due to the spirits and their interest in us, our well being and our lives. I love that part the most. Being a servitor of Vodou means being part of the great cosmos on an intimate scale.

So the question now is – where do you go from here? Having started down this rabbit hole, you probably want to know where it leads. Well, it leads to you. Vodou begins with your Ancestors. I always tell my students "find out about yourself." It is not hard or scary. And it is the core of the Vodou Faith. No one ever questions my role as a mambo. They always say, "You do Vodou? Where is your family from? Where is your demambre (land) located?" My Ancestors are the key to my living and working as a Mambo Asogwe. There is no getting around it either, as I am constantly reminded.

Karen McCarthy Brown has said, "If you're in, you're in." and that means, if you are kanzo, then you are in the club for life. And with that membership comes a heap of responsibilities. The first responsibility is all about remembering and serving your ancestors. Remembrance is the heart and soul of Vodou. This responsibility to remember the ancestors begins long before anyone should kanzo. It is the footprint and foundation of all Vodou work. Accepting who you are and working with your family is the way toward harmony and balance. And let's remember that balance and harmony are the key to being a Vodouisant.

Your ancestors wait with infinite patience for you to find your way to them. Didn't like old weird Uncle Al? That is ok. Where was Uncle Al from? Italy, Romania, China? Those are your Ancestors. Study their history, figure out what they ate, what music they listened to and what kind of clothes they wore. Then, craft your Ancestor altar to that culture. Have family from Ireland? Then play Irish music, make an altar cloth with Celtic knots, bake some scones and serve them Irish Breakfast tea, and sit. And wait. Be patient. It is not a race, it is a marathon. Do this monthly and see if your Ancestors don't come calling.

Talk to your family. Having lost my parents, I no longer have that resource for things like old family names, family stories. Even identifying pictures is lost to us now. So speak up. Put aside the petty issues. Get over yourself and go speak to the elders of your family. Take a moment to find out the wondrous or funny or just plain old dumb tales that are hidden in your family's skeleton closet. I assure you, they are worth finding out about. Because hidden inside those stories are clues to your history, clues as to who you are and why you do the things you do.

The Lwa are the most like us. We are the most like the Lwa. Want to know who your constellation is? Then take the time to find out who your family is, because they will mirror the Lwa in that walk with you in your life.

Like draws to Like. We are not so different from our heavenly family. They come to us because we are exactly like them. Fragile. Frightened. Full of mischief and love. They are attracted to us, with all our issues and faults and foibles, because they recognize themselves in us. And they still love us. These great energies that can move between heaven and earth, choose to walk with us here and now. If that doesn't make you feel special, then I don't know what would.

Begin to do Vodou by learning about yourself, learning about your family and you can't go wrong. That is because the Ancestors know what is needed. I know I have said this already, but it bears repeating here. Your Ancestors are the living parts of your family tree who were strong enough to survive the plagues, infections and dangers of their time. They were healthy enough to have children, and wise enough to learn how to raise them in an ever changing world. They have the tools you need to live your life here and now. So find time to talk to them. They just might surprise you.

Small, steady, consistent efforts always yield the best results, so keep your steps small at first. Find out about your ancestors. Find a reputable Vodou house and see if you can attend their services and speak to the Lwa. Ask questions. A good house will always be ready to talk and share their knowledge. And commit to being a balanced, cool headed person. In doing so, you will go a long way to finding your footing in Vodou.

As a further aid, I have included a bibliography, a reading list and some additional information that can help broaden your horizons in Vodou. Read broadly, sing lustily and dance whenever you can. I assure you, you are not alone.

The great Lwa walk with you every day. They are a ready resource, willing to reach down through the veils of time and space to lend a hand whenever you call upon them. They do not care if you sing off key or can only find time to offer a glass of water. They are omnipresent, timeless and spiritually available to all of us. They listen with openness to all Their servitors, respond with love, forgive our faults and delight in our efforts. They do not choose among us nor do They see us as apart from Themselves. Rather They see us as a part of Themselves. They walk with all of us because Vodou includes, it does not exclude. Ayibobo.

Resources

I read everything I can find on Vodou - the good and the bad. The following listing is by no means comprehensive or exhaustive. These are the books I that have read and found to have worthy or accurate information on Vodou. They are listed in the bibliography with their publishers for your reference.

Esoteric Vodou Reading List:

Many people want to know where the theology is in Vodou. During the 30s and 40s, there was a resurgence of interest in the effect Africa had on Haiti. Many notable literati of Haitian society wrote beautiful books on many subjects. The greatest wealth of knowledge about Vodou and its African theology came out of this time frame. These are my top choices.

Le Tradition Voudou et Le Voudou Haitien by Milo Rigaud Paris 1953 In French, 430 pages. There is a shorter English version titled Secrets of Voodoo. If you find the French, I would say go for that first. Otherwise, the English version is good, just missing some major thoughts and ideas.

Vèvè- Diagrammes Rituels du Vodou - Milo Rigaud in English, French and Spanish - still in print, and an excellent resource on the vèvès of Haitian Vodou.

Les Daimons du Cult Vodou- Arthur Holly (Her-Ma-Ra-el)1918 Paris. You can download a pdf version of the entire book at the University of Florida's on-line Latin American Collection here: http://ufdc.ufl.edu/UF00077416/00001/thumbs

Rigaud and Holly both were members of secret societies within Vodou and were also Masons. That is why their books have an esoteric turn.

Secrets of Vodou by Milo Riguad, 1969. The English edition of the above mentioned one. This is an excellent review of Vodou by the Haitian born writer.

Dancing Spirits: Rhythms and Rituals of Haitian Vodun, the Rada Rite by Gerdes Fleurant 1996

A Haitian emigrant goes back to his roots to learn the Drum and be initiated. Mr. Fleurant is a college professor in the Boston area. Good information on the Bonpo area of Haiti.

Divine Horsemen by Maya Deren. 1954. This is still the classic text on Haitian Vodou. Deren went to Haiti to film the dances, but initiated into the faith, placed her camera and films in a trunk and promptly forgot all about them. She did write this amazing book that recounts her time in Haiti, what she learned and how it all comes together. Her description of possession is a classic.

Fragments of Bone by Patrick Bellegarde-Smith.2005 University of Illinois Press. Bellegarde-Smith draws on an impressive range of sources including research, fieldwork, personal interviews, and spiritual introspection. Examining the theology, cosmology, rituals and their sociopolitical contexts, the authors demonstrate that the African ethos behind the religions of Vodou, Santeria as well as Candomble, Lukumi, and Palomonte remains true to the original theological beliefs of the ancestral practices.

Haitian Vodou: Spirit, Myth and Reality, edited by Patrick Bellgarde-Smith and Claudine Michel, 2006 Indiana University Press. A book on Haitian Vodou by Haitians. It contains ten essays ranging from the herbs of Vodou to the theological implications of Vodou on Haitian politics.

Invisible Powers: Vodou in Haitian Life and Culture, edited by Patrick Bellgarde-Smith and Claudine Michel. 2006 Palgrave MacMillian Publishing. Another compilation of excellent essays by the same pair of scholars. This time, the focus is on the culture of Vodou as expressed trough art, dance, music and literature. An excellent insight into the details of Vodou.

Alan Lomax's Recordings in Haiti, liner notes by Gage Averil. 2009, Harte Recordings, LLC. Liner notes is misleading. This hard cover book is 164 pages of songs, translations, interpretations, history and clues to the world of Vodou. It is included in the 10 CD set of Alan Lomax in Haiti.

For Art Lovers:

Art and Vodou go together like *riz ak dwi* (rice and peas). Some of the best information about Vodou can be gleaned from these books:

Sacred Arts of Haitian Vodou by Donald J. Cosentino, editor 1995. A beautiful art book and a feast for the eyes. I saw the exhibit in

1995, when it came to the Baltimore Art Museum. Along with a gaggle of gorgeous photos, it contains an excellent collection of essays by leading scholars, Mambos and Houngans. This is the real Vodou, not a mishmash of nonsense.

Sequin Artists of Haiti by Tina Girouard 1994 . The first and original books on the sequin flags (called drapos) of Haitian Vodou. Tina worked with Antoine Oleyant, the master flag maker of Haiti and this book is their story. It is an intimate look at the drapo makers of Bel Air, with lots of good information about the making of drapo, the meaning behind the beads and quite a few funny stories on friends of the sosyete.

Vodou: Visions and Voices of Haiti, Phyllis Galembo, Ten Speed Press, 2005. Photographer Phyllis Galembo shows us the human and divine faces and voices of real Haitian Vodou as it is practiced today.

Spirits in Sequins by Nancy Josephson. Schiffer Books, 2007.. The book explores the spiritual beliefs at the core of the designs and the folk lore expressed in this unique format. A little history of Haiti and a little explanation of the Vodou religion helps to explain the people who create these flags.

Vodou, a Way of Life. Jacques Hainard, Phillippe Mathez and Olivier Schinz, eds. Infolio/Musee d 'ethnographic de Genève, 2008. Stunning art catalog with 20 essays on the amazing Bizango collection of Madame Marianne Lehman. Rachel Beauvoir-

Dominique adds her illuminating words to the catalogue with current ideas and new thoughts on the history of Vodou.

Appendix

Here are some charts worth having, to help learn the correspondences of the Lwa. If you didn't grow up Catholic, it'll be easier to figure out who the saints are and why they syncretize with the Lwa.

Lwa Name	Saint Correspondence	Shared symbolism
Legba	Saint Peter	For the keys to heaven
	St. Anthony	The wanderer
	Saint Lazarus	For the crutches
Marassa	Sts.Cosmos and Damian	They are twins
Loko	Saint Joseph	Father figure
Ayizan	Saint Claire	The host she holds
Danbala	Saint Patrick	Snakes under feet
Ayida Wedo	Our Lady of Conception	Multi-color cherubs

Agwe	St. Ulrich	The fish in hand
LaSirenn	Diosa del Mar Stella Maris	Lady in the sea Virgin with seven stars
Erzulie Freda	Our Lady of Mount Calvary	All the jewelry
Azaka Mede	Saint Isidore	Plowing a field
Ogoun	Sts. Michael, Elais, George, Expedite	All soldiers with swords
Bossou	Triple Ray Christos St.Vincent de Paul	Triple horns Protector of Innocents
Legba Petro	Saint Anthony	The miracle worker
Marassa Petro	Three Virtues	Twins, plus Dosu/Dosa
Ezili Dantor	Our Lady of Czestochowa	Black Madonna with child
The Simbis	Three Magi	For their magical powers

The Baron	Saint Martin de Porres	Black priest in black robes
Maman Brijit	St. Bridget	Name correlation only.
Guédé Nibo	Saint Gerard Majeur	The skull and cross

Web Sites

I always feel looking for information on the internet is like an extended game of scavenger hunt. It is at best an overgrown path with many false trails. These sites have been up for five years, contain real information and are worth your time surfin.' Enjoy.

www.sosyetedumarche.com. The house web site, with an extensive library of articles, pages on the major Lwa and class links. An excellent resource for your studies.

http://www.indigoarts.com/gallery_haiti_main.html. A gallery that specializes in Caribbean and Haitian artworks, located here in Philadelphia, PA. Some of the books in the bibliography can be purchased here.

http://www.vodou.org/. Papa Max Beauvoir's temple located in Marianni, Haiti. Excellent articles, and the definitive list of herbs used in Vodou, with scientific, Creole and Spanish names.

http://thelouvertureproject.org   This site is dedicated to Toussaint L'Ouverture who led the revolution for Haiti is freedom. There is history here you won't find in other books. Read about people like Cecil Fatiman, the infamous mambo of Bwa Caiman; a true history of Boukman and find out who Makandal really was. Interesting history, legendary heroes and other information on Haiti can be found here.

http://rara.wesleyan.edu/ Liza McAlister's ongoing web site about the Rara of Haiti. Liza spent time all over the country, studying the Rara bands as they "walked". She returned with miles of footage, many photos and great recordings of all the songs. The web site is rich in pictures, video clips, and excerpts from her book.

http://www.michaelventura.org/writings/EB2.pdf. Ventura's essay about the influence of Vodou on the music industry today. Written in 1987, it is still fresh and relevant. (Many thanks to the Tambor for this one).

http://surrealdocuments.blogspot.com/2008/11/vodou-art-and-mysticism-from-haiti.html.   An interesting blog about Marianne Lehman's Bizango Collection show in the Netherlands. It has photos from the galleries showing the many articles and items in the collection, with links to the museum that sponsored the show

Bibliography

Ackerman, H., Gautier, M., Momplaisir, M.A. (2011). *Les Esprit du Vodou* Haitien. Coconut Creek, FL: Educa Vision Inc.

Anglade, P. (1998). *Inventaire etymologique des termes creoles des caraibes d'origine africain.* Paris: L'harmattan.

Basden, G. T. (2008). *Among the Ibos of Nigeria.* Ann Arbor, MI: UMI Microform 3297540.

Bastide, R.. (1972). *African Civilisations in the New World.* London: C.Hurst and Company Publishers Ltd.

Bay, E. (1998). *Wives of the Leopard: gender, politics and culture in the Kingdom of Dahomey.* Charlottesville, VA: University of Virginia Press.

Beauvoir-Dominique, R. (2007). The vodou-makaya artistic tradition in haiti's heritage. In Mathez, P. & Hainard, J. (Ed.), *Vodou: A Way of Life* (pp. 167-174). Genève: Infolio/Musée d'ethnographie de Genèva.

Bellegarde-Smith, P., & Michel, C. (Ed.). (2006). *Haitian Vodou: Spirit, Myth and Reality.* Bloomington, IN: Indiana University Press.

Bellegarde-Smith, P., & Michel, C. (Ed.). (2006). *Invisible Powers: Vodou in Haitian Life and Culture.* New York, NY: Palgrave,MacMillan.

Daniel, Y. (2005). *Dancing Wisdom: Embodied Knowledge in Haitian Vodou, Cuban Yoruba and Bahain Candomble.* University of Illinois Press.

Davis, W. (1997). *The Serpent and the Rainbow.* Clearwater, FL:Touchstone

Desmangles, L. (1992). *The Faces of the Gods*. Chapel Hill: The University of North Carolina Press.

Emmanuel, P. (1962). *Panorama du Folklore Haitien*, preface africiane en Haiti. Port-au-Prince, Haiti: Imprimerie de l'Etat.

Ferere, G. A. (1989). *Le Vouduisme Haitien*. Philadelphia, PA: Saint Joseph University Press.

Fleurant, G. (1996). *Dancing Spirits*. Westport, CT: Greenwood Press.

Fouchard, J. (1981). *The Haitian Marroons: Liberty of Death*. Brooklyn, NY: Blyden.

Gilles, J. (2009). *Roots, Rituals, Remembrance*. Davie, FL: Bookmanlit.

Guigard, M.F. (2006). *La Legende de Loa*. Miami, FL: ReMe Art Publishing.

Girouard, T. (1994). *Sequin Artists of Haiti*. New Orleans, LA. Contemporary Arts Center.

Heinl, N.G. & Heinl, R.D. (1996). *Written in Blood: the Story of the Haitian People*. Lanham, MD: University Press of America

Herskovitts, M. (1958). *Dahomean Narrative: a cross-cultural analysis*. Evanston, IL: Northwestern University Press.

Houlberg, M. (2005). The ritual cosmos of the twins. In P. Bellegarde-Smith (Ed.), *Fragments of Bone: neo-African religions in a new world* (pp. 13-31). Urbana: University of Illinois Press.

(2011). Two equals three. In P Peek (Ed.), *Twins in African and Diaspora Cultures: Double Trouble, Twice Blessed* (pp. 271-289). Bloomington: Indiana University Press.

Hutton, C. (1821) *The Tour of Africa.* London: Baldwin, Cradock and Joy.

Jennings, LaVinia D.. (2008). *Toni Morrison and the idea of Africa*. Cambridge, UK: Cambridge University Press.

LaGuerre, M. S. (1980). *Voodoo Heritage*. New York, NY: Sage Publications, Inc. 1980

Larose, S. (1977). *Symbols and Sentiments: Cross Cultural Studies in Symbolism*. London : Academic Press, Inc.

Lovejoy, P. (2000). *Transformation in Slavery*. Cambridge: Cambridge University Press.

McAlister, L. (2002). *Rara! Vodou, Power and Performance in Haiti*. Berkeley: University of California Press.

Mclean, F. (2008, January 01). The lost fort of columbus. *Smithsonian Magazine*, Retrieved from http://www.smithsonianmag.com/history-archaeology/fort-of-columbus-200801.html.

Manning, P. (1993). Migrations of africans to the americas the impact on africans, africa and the new world. *The History Teacher*, 26(3), 279-296.

MacGaffery, W. (1983). *Modern Kongo Prophets: Religion in a Plural Society*. Bloomington, IN: Indiana University Press.

Marcelin, M. (1949). *Mythologie Vodou (Rite Arada)*. 2 Volumes. Port-au_prince, Haiti: Les Editions Haitiennes.

Martinie, Louis. (1986). *Waters of Return: The Aeonic Flow of Voudoo*. Cincinnati: Black Moon Publishing.

Martinie, L. & Glassman, S. (1996) *The New Orleans Voodoo Tarot*. Stamford, CT: U.S. Games Systems, Inc.

McCarthy-Brown, K. (2001). *Mama Lola.* Berkeley: University of California Press.

Paul, Emmanuel C. (1962) *Panorama du folklore haitien.* Port-au-Prince: Imprimerie de l'Etat.

Price-Mars, J., trans. Shannon, M. (1983). *So Spoke the Uncle.* Washington DC: Three Continents Press.

Richman, K. (2008). *Vodou and Migration.* Gainesville: University Press of Florida.

Rigaud, M. (1969). *Secrets of Vodou.* New York: Arco Publishing (1974) *Voodoo Diagrams & Rituals.* New York: French & Euroepean Publications

Robinson, D. (2004). *Muslin Societies in African History.* New York: Cambridge University Press.

Rodman, S. (1988). *Where Art is Joy.* New York, NY:Rules de Latour

Rogozinski, J. (1999). *A Brief History of the Caribbean* (Revised ed.). New York: Facts on File, Inc

Saint-Lot, M.J.A. (2003). *Vodou A Sacred Theater.* Coconut Creek, FL: Educa Vision Inc.

Sharkey, N. (1988, December 11). A barbados synagogue is reborn. Retrieved from *http://www.nytimes.com/1988/12/11/travel/a-barbados-synagogue-is-reborn.html*

Sheridan, R. (1994). *Sugar and Slavery: An Economic History of the British West Indies, 1623-1775.* Kingston, Jamaica: University of the West Indies Press

Thornton, John. (1998). *Africa and Africans in the Making of the Atlantic World 1400-1800.* Cambridge: Cambridge University Press.
(1998). *The Kongo Saint Anthony: Dona Beatriz Kimpa Vita and the Antonian Movement, 1684-1706.* Cambridge: Cambridge University Press.

Vansina, J. Bells of Kings, *The Journal of African History*, Volume 10, Number 2, 1969, pages 187-197

Winddrum, S. (2005). *African Initiations: Rites of Passage through the Eyes of an Initiate.* Philadelphia, PA: Borders Personal Publishing

Index

Abomey, 110. 135, 204

Abysmal Waters, 64, 75, 207, 262

Adja, 110, 129, 159

affranchis, 29-30, 51

Agarou, 71

Agassou, 15, 71,107, 110, 140

Agbe, 140, 145

Agwe Tawayo, 71, 98, 101, 141, 148, 201

agwesans, 66

Aida, 71, 110, 135, 137, 215

Aida Hwedo, 135

Aida Wedo, 135

Alada, 140

Alarada, 61, 229

altar, 11.4144.67.66.93-94.01, 114, 124, 142, 146, 153, 156, 169, 175, 192, 202, 218, 221, 237, 263, 270, 276

Amerindians, 64

Anais-Anais, 45, 153, 155

Anba Dlo, 62, 246, 247, 260, 262

ancestors, 14,57, 63 ,75, 78, 80, 83, 86, 87-89, 93-94, 102-105, 114, 119, 129, 135-136, 162, 186, 191-193, 198, 200-204, 207, 212, 220, 224, 226, 245, 248, 250-251, 255, 262, 264, 275-277

Arawak, 23- 25, 37, 129, 159, 161

Aries, 170

Artibonite, 38, 57, 183, 242

ashe, 178, 192, 193, 222, 265, 269

Asogwe, 66, 93, 219, 221, 223, 238, 256, 268, 270, 275

asson, 37, 105, 128-130, 175, 194, 222, 231, 233, 236-239, 261

authority, 91, 93, 125, 204, 233-234

Avelekete, 118

Ayizan, 58, 71, 110, 132-134, 201, 225, 255, 284

Velekete, 132

Azaka Mede, 78, 154, 159, 194, 202, 285

Aziri, 145, 148, 152, 181

Azor, 42-43

Bade, 71, 110, 125, 126, 139, 169

badji, 112, 137, 218, 219

Badjio, 39

bak d'Agwe, 141

banda, 205

Baron

   Cimetière, 205, 208

   Kriminel, 208

   La Croix, 205, 207

Mambo Vye Zo Komande La Menfo

Patricia Scheu (Mambo Vye Zo Komande LaMenfo) studied graphic design at the University of Connecticut. A love of Haitian artwork led her to Jacmel, where she was ordained as a Mambo Asogwe. She and her husband currently lead Sosyete du Marche, Inc., a 501c3 Vodou church in Pennsylvania. Ordained as a "mother of the spirits" in Haiti 2003, she tirelessly promotes the Vodou faith. She serves the spirits through education, public speaking and ceremony. Her story and artwork are at www.sosyetedumarche.com. Photo by D.M. Scheu.

15454897R00163

Made in the USA
Lexington, KY
29 May 2012